THE HUNTER'S WAY

DEY ST.
An Imprint of WILLIAM MORROW

The

HUNTER'S

WAY

A GUIDE TO THE
HEART AND SOUL OF HUNTING

CRAIG RALEIGH

DEY ST.

HarperCollins books may be purchased for educational, business, or sales promotional use. For information, please email the Special Markets Department at SPsales@harpercollins.com.

FIRST EDITION

Designed by Michelle Crowe
Title page art by Ivan Baranov/ Shutterstock, Inc.
Animal illustrations by andrey oleynik, pixpenart/ Shutterstock, Inc.
Part opener backgrounds by immstudio, N K, Mark Bridger, jo crebbin/ Shutterstock, Inc.

Library of Congress Cataloging-in-Publication Data has been applied for.

ISBN 978-0-06-283932-9

18 19 20 21 22   RS/LSC   10 9 8 7 6 5 4 3 2 1

FOR STEVE BRIAN PRATT

U.S. Army SPC 4th Class
458th Trans. Co.
PBR
Sea Tigers, Saigon River
Vietnam 1968–69
July 5, 1948 ~ June 2, 2016
Invited everyone, asked nothing, and wanted only
to hunt with his family and friends.

It was on his property that I wrote most of this book.

CONTENTS

AUTHOR'S NOTE

Throughout the text I use the pronoun "he" when describing hunters. This is only a stylistic element and it by no means expresses a belief that all hunters are male. Au contraire, I've seen some enviable hunters of all genders, shapes, and sizes.

PREFACE

Whether we want to admit it, we are all hunters. The emotional and physical chase—and the reward that may or may not come from it—is the bread and butter of human instinct. Let's face it, no longer do most people have to physically hunt in order to gain life-giving proteins, but it is by doing so that we embody characteristics like honesty, respect, persistence, and humility. It's the hunters' respect for the creatures we know and love that has led to honorable trades like veterinary and animal husbandry, and it's one of the larger reasons we began to domesticate the animals we hunted and bring them closer to our sights. Men and women have partnered throughout time to obtain food, clothing, and shelter by way of the hunt. We live and breathe the rules of the fair chase in order to survive in a world that gives no quarter and takes no prisoners.

As important as hunting success in early history was, the celebration that came afterward was even more profound. Families greeted accomplishment with the understanding that the hunt wasn't only necessary for survival but was a deeply ingrained way of meeting after the harvest and giving thanks for all that they had. Similarly, we have lived and thrived by the hunt and have found its continued existence necessitated by an honorable system in which the hunter gladly accepts the role of provider; no longer do humans survive merely by the innate ability to fend off disease or by gathering what they could find by scavenging.

Once evolution had taken hold, the hunter was unleashed. Sticks and stones were replaced by spears and bows; the discovery of fire was as good for bodily warmth as it was for cooking meat. Humans went from gatherers to hunters and in the process learned to dominate their surroundings. It was then, even in the early days of human existence, that they began to care for the earth like no other creature could. The hunt is where we became conscious and reasoned animals; it is where we discovered our destiny of noble conservationist—where we assumed our roll as overseer of the environment and landlord to the world, for better or worse.

◆

I have spent most of my life outdoors trying to find that elusive Holy Grail, that reality of hunting where pleasure combines with practice. It's not just the dream of catching a giant northern pike or muskellunge, or dropping one's very first pheasant; it's not meeting the buck's wide-eyed gaze and anticipating the right trajectory in which expertise meets precision. It's something deeper than that.

Thanks to my father and grandfather, I've had the outdoors on my mind (and on my boots' treads) since I was a little boy. This "mobile life" has afforded me every opportunity to create for myself the kind of robust love for nature that anyone can imagine and a respect for all forms of life that one could ever name. A life lived in the outdoors is massively rewarding, offers nonstop pleasures, and provides the ultimate in appreciation of the natural world. It offers camaraderie, freedom of choice, and reward, and to that end it never stops giving. I am part of the hunting community, and no one loves the great outdoors quite like we do. We come to it in our souls and defend it with our hearts. We dare to wait on stands in lonesome trees and walk through smelly swamps. The earth on our hands and faces is the badge of honor we wear proudly. There is no greater appreciation for something than to carry its scent with you. My dog had it—she carried it with us everywhere we went. Not something abhorrent, or disgusting, nay, familiar and glad. It was a unique trace of her that I knew immediately, and if I could have kept it in a bottle to cheer me up when she was gone, I would have.

The hunt is so much more than the kill. The hunter often

walks away from the woods and fields empty-handed. Some see in this a profound beauty, while others find disappointment and shame. Regardless of the result, a hunter must be prepared to return and repeat the process of observation necessary for success.

While finding a good hunting spot is certainly not the same as, say, finding your keys, both start with the same methodology: *Where's the likeliest place to start looking? What would the best "sign" be? Have I seen them in this spot last time I lost them?* In nature, however, the clues are changeable and never the same the second time. For example, a buck will use common trails throughout the season but might be drawn off course by the scent of a hot doe; grouse that once flushed off the ground are now rocketing from the pine trees.

Hunting is a pause on the path of life—an opportunity to see, smell, and appreciate all that we get from spending a lifetime as outdoorsmen. It takes time, practice, dedication, and effort, and it's in these traits that we find our true selves: We are not as concerned with what we can take from the world as we are with the prospect of what it delivers to us in the first place. As such, we are constantly thinking about how to give back. That kind of work is never finished.

This book is filled with examples of the hunter's place in nature—from the banal to the comical to the extreme. But it's also about that intangible, meditative feeling that the outdoors provides us. The hunter sees every tree in every yard and begins to identify birds flying by. We don't just notice the sunrise, we know exactly what time it happens. We are the ones who post the meteor shower times and dates on social media. We walk outside in the pouring rain just to smell it. We love to stand on the deck in the freezing cold to look at the stars, and we can tell you where the constellations lie. We understand that every twig that bends back and slaps our faces, every thorn that sinks into our skin, is just a reminder that nature rules the planet, not the humans that inhabit it. Our signpost is the leafless tree; our painting the cirrus clouds in the sky. We do not grieve for those who do not share in this enthusiasm for the hunt but smile in the face of its adversity. We are disciples of nature and of the great outdoors. We have advanced degrees in gratitude for this good earth and where it is that everything comes from. Our shared inner peace comes from a mind-set of grace and dignity, of knowing that the earth was here long before us and will be here long after we have gone.

Finding common ground is the reason for a book about hunting. I wouldn't try and persuade a nonhunter into becoming that which he may despise, the same way I wouldn't care to be told I'm an inhuman monster because I hunt. The contents herein are meant as a call to those with a unique sense of the surrounding earth and its vast pleasures. My only hope is that nonhunters may see us in a different light, or else are as beckoned to the great outdoors as much as we are.

The second that I sit down to write about the outdoors, I immediately feel the urge to get up and go out there. (I start to feel rather lazy if I don't!) Putting this desire into words is one of my callings, and I hope yours is to take lessons from this book and go outside with a newfound appreciation and an open heart. I hope you read this book under a big oak tree or in a canoe treading soft waves. I hope you find solace and purpose in its lessons, and see the hunter in a robust new light.

Part One

THE BACKGROUND

We do not have to be ashamed of what we are. As sentient beings we have wonderful backgrounds. These backgrounds may not be particularly enlightened or peaceful or intelligent. Nevertheless, we have soil good enough to cultivate; we can plant anything in it.

—CHÖGYAM TRUNGPA,
Cutting Through Spiritual Materialism

MYTHOLOGY OF THE HUNTER'S EGO

A story:

I have a friend Mike—my best friend's cousin—who prefers to stand on the ground as opposed to in a tree during our deer drives, those doggedly simple brush-busting operations that move sitting deer from one area to another with the prospect of the almighty barbecue awaiting on the far end.

It's not because he's afraid of heights but because he says he's a better hunter on the ground. Mind you, Mike is a six-foot-something, 280-pound ex–football player and former army corporal who likes to chew tobacco and demolish adult beverages with impunity. He wears a blaze-orange coat that has such an odd camouflage pattern that we call it cow-camo because of its resemblance to a cow's hide. His physical presence isn't fooling anyone, least of all those nimble deer.

Hunting with him requires talking him into getting up in the tree stand overlooking the opening where the deer always pop out. We remind him that if we let him stand on the ground, the tall grass will be in the way of his shot; it's also much safer to be up in that permanent tree fort that we built.

One afternoon in November, following the usual short lecture, we got him to climb into the tree stand, and off the rest of us went to set the drive in motion.

After a grueling forty-five-minute walk through intensely thick cover, Mike's low voice crackled over our radios: "I've got deer moving toward me."

Five minutes passed, during which we waited for the deer to respond and make their move toward this massive friend of ours. Then we heard him unload all five shots out of his 12-gauge. Those of us walking the drive wondered to ourselves just how many deer would be lying there when we reached him. *Three? Four?*

When we arrived back at the stand, Mike was already on the ground. No deer. No blood at his feet. No hair anywhere from a near miss. Most surprising was the guffaw he let loose as soon as we reached his position. One of us asked him if he had even seen a deer, to which he answered uproariously, "Yeah, there were five of them! I missed all five times, and probably could've reloaded, but I ran out of shells. I told you that I should've stayed on the ground!"

"So we pushed the gravy train right by you, and you missed everything?" I asked.

"I didn't know which one to shoot at."

"Any of the ones with four legs would've been good," I said.

Maybe he should have stayed on the ground. Or maybe we were right by putting him up in that tree, based on our experience in this location. All I know is that from that day forward—and we christened the area the "gravy train spot" because of this very incident, as well as the fact that we always found deer moving there—one couldn't be sure of anything.

Laughing is a part of our defense system, the final round in the holster. When I heard "I've got deer moving toward me," I imagined Mike's excitement, paired with the anxiety of a fish-in-a-barrel complex. I imagined him telling himself: *Missing is no big deal.* Or: *Maybe they won't even come this way,* as if to prepare himself for the worst. Laughter, it seems, was all he had left.

Contrary to this are the experienced hunters whose egos are fully enlarged. Their uncertainty is confidence, their failure success. They are the ones who will usually find ways to brag about their harvest, or who will take a lifetime to achieve any skills worth sharing. The one thing their egos won't let them do is admit it.

———◆———

Even though hunters are unique in their individual styles, the goal is a common one: to harvest the deer or other game. But finding what works best for each of us gives rise to many forms of methodology and, of course, debate.

While one hunter's technique to take ducks on the lakeshore may include the specifics of how he sets out his block of decoys, another has a surefire gimmick that he's certain works better. Naturally, this is fine. All of us revel in our own styles, habits, and techniques; and if they work, why give them up? It's not that the hunter wants to keep his ideas to himself but that he has the desire to make his way known as the *best way*. The hunter reveals his techniques for many reasons, but bragging rights are prominent among them.

Case in point: I have another friend, Tommy, with whom I've hunted deer for years. He likes to use a portable tree-climbing stand to put different areas of the woods closer in his sights, moving it around before and especially during the season like the rest of us. One year in particular the woods in our area abounded with tales of hunters whose equipment had gone missing; mysteriously "growing legs" and walking out of the forest all by itself.

Since Tom is about as trusting and cynical as any of us who've had something stolen, he doesn't like knowing that his stand may disappear, even with a padlock on it, so here was his solution: He left his climber twenty feet up in the tree.

And each time he hunts, he climbs up the tree trunk to use his stand or retrieve it, thus defeating its purpose. He is as nimble as a gazelle and never misses the chance to let us know it. *He can out-wrestle, out-hunt, and, obviously, out-climb any of us.* The thing is, he doesn't need to use his climbing trick as proof of this; nor does he need to shout it from the treetops.

Sometimes the brag is encapsulated in unusual quirks.

Another example: I hunted with a man who was a veteran home builder and another who used to be my brother-in-law. Both were, in their day, avid deer hunters who climbed trees and sat for the entire day waiting for that big buck to pass by. The difference between them and many like them I've met is their use of a lit cigar to attract said big buck.

My former brother-in-law learned this technique while hunting on a hillside in southern New York State. He would swear that the burning smoke would waft down the hill and that trophy deer would come running up after it. His cigar of choice was a Backwoods Smoke, a refreshingly sweet and aromatic little slice of joy that can stink a skunk out of its den. He wouldn't just swear by this method; no, he would chortle at anyone who didn't believe it, flaunting the trophy hanging above his mantel as proof. "Without it," he'd say, "you're not going to see a thing."

The land that the veteran builder was hunting at that time was parkland, sold off to make room for the homes that now look as if they've been there forever. Some of the many deer that they harvested in that area (long before the homes encroached on it) only had dealings with human beings who were walking their dogs, jogging, or, as fate would have it, out to have a cigar. He told me about a time when he set his smoke down to take a pee off the side of the stand, which actually made it easier for him to pick up his bow (yes, his bow!) and draw back in time to double-lung a giant ten-pointer that was standing directly below him.

Currently above his mantel is a beautiful head mount of that trophy ten-pointer. Since then, the cigar has remained a staple.

This style of hunting is nothing to laugh about. Many outdoor brands have begun to make products that burn, smoke, waft, spray, and otherwise leave an airborne scent trail for miles. Some of my friends swear by these products, while others wonder how a deer can tell where the smoke is coming from. Perhaps even stranger than this methodology is what my friend Tom with the tree stand says about catching the deer's nose in this fashion: "It all depends on the direction of the thermals based on the moon phase."

I tell him to let me know when the planets align.

———•———

Now, when it comes to the inevitable deer drive, everyone's an expert. If you ask one person you may as well ask ten because you will get ten different answers. I've seen hunting parties that set out into the woods with a manpower drive of twenty men or more. It will certainly make the deer move, but as an "expert" method it leaves a lot to be desired. Other times, I've been in a tree when ten guys went by yelling their heads off; the only thing they didn't have were pots and pans to bang on (or deer because they were all in the next county).

But since folks are still using these madcap methods, it stands to reason that they've had some success with them. They're everywhere: guys in a duck blind on the shore of a large lake waving white hankies like they were surrendering (a precursor to today's well-known method of flagging and the flapper decoys). Most hunters believe that rattling antlers together can bring a big buck running toward them ready to fight, and others claim that hooting an owl call at the end of the evening will make a big boss Tom turkey gobble and give away his roosting position up in the treetops. It seems that so many of the successful techniques that we now use once began as somebody's zany idea. I mean, at some point a hunter somewhere in antiquity talked himself into spreading a deer's urine on himself, and the rest is history. Did you know that in some parts of Scotland they hunt for flounder at low tide by removing their shoes and . . . *tramping them with their feet?* Onward . . .

Bragging takes on many shapes, sizes, and colors. Once,

while Tom and I were deer hunting a friend's farm in the southern part of Monroe County, in New York, we happened upon a father and son duo that had been using the property for many years. They hadn't actually ever asked the owners for permission, but they were former employees of the farm so it was unspoken knowledge that they were welcome. The first time we talked with them was while meeting to put on a push around lunchtime. The father was amiable but effusive on his methodology:

"Now, what we're going to do is head down to the lane at the far end of the property. When we get there we're going to start at a small oak tree. Not any oak tree, it's the one that Buddy planted when he was a kid. He said that it was grown from an acorn that his mom had given him. Now, his mom never hunted, but his dad's stand is the best one out here. It's not made of oak, you see, but it's been there for a long time and he still uses it. About ten years ago I saw a big buck rubbing it while it was still a sapling. I couldn't get a shot off at that big baysterd, but I scared the bejeczus outta him and I never seen him again!" (*Yes, he said "bay-sterd."*)

We sat listening to this mess of a story and realized that he hadn't told us anything substantial about the hunt except that he had once chased a big buck out of the county. My friend and I looked at each other and held it together long enough for him to continue.

". . . What we'll do is we'll start over there and walk up the edge to the cattails. Now, them cattails is tall, mind you. You can get lost in that stuff, but that's where the deer lay, right in there. One time when we was making this push the pond in the middle was full of mallards. You never heard so much noise. We was wishing we had brung some birdshot with us!"

I had to interrupt him. I hardly know the man, but that's my temperament. Trust me, sometimes it pays to unclog your speaking filter and just let it out. "Are you actually going to go down there and do it, or just tell us about it?"

Tom let out one of those stifling laughs like when you try to suppress a sneeze. Still, the father didn't stop talking:

"Now, sometimes a fox will squirt outta there, you know, so be ready for a fox. I seen a big one down at Fred's place the other day. It was all mangy and beat-up looking. Fred doesn't have chickens anymore so I just don't know why a fox would be down there. We used to trap them down at Miller's Creek. We would get five bucks a pelt in them days . . ."

It took us going silent and walking away before the son of a gun realized how much he was prattling on. By then he was anything but embarrassed; I don't even think he knew what being embarrassed was, although his son did, judging from his face.

The father finally relented. "Okay, we're going to head down there if you want to set up down along the hedgerow here," he said.

Tom and I walked west down that very same hedgerow—a sparse, elongated island of leftover cover that stretched out east and west along the edge of a cut cornfield on the north side and separated by a few yards from cut beans on the south. Toward the woods we traveled to spread out and set up, while the father and son began their journey south toward the marshes to turn and work their way back north.

It was a late-season hunt and the whitetails weren't going to move unless we moved them. Tom and I set up in competing spots along the hedgerow—looking south toward the cattails—with at least 100 or 150 yards between us. Think of a huge, east-west rectangle that is extremely long, maybe 400 to 450 yards—easily as long as a tough par four on any good golf course. The benefit of this orientation is that it is wide open, and since there were only four of us it was easy to pick out blaze-orange vests from fleeing deer.

Now, I understand that those two guys pushing and the two of us waiting on stand isn't the most ideal deer-drive hunting situation, but we've had success with hard luck circumstances before, so we took it for what it was. We just couldn't have expected to see what we watched the father and son do next.

One of them had taken the long walk down to the eastern edge of the beanfield, while the other went down to the far western edge, and then both started to walk south. When they got to their respective spots and the end of the field bordering the cattails—which ran the entire length of the beanfield—we expected them to disappear into the cover and keep going south, so that they could walk back through the mass of cattails toward us in a northerly direction. The father stopped at the southwest corner of the beans, and the son put the brakes on at the southeast corner. With each one in a corner of the field in plain sight of each other, they stared down the ends of the field, gave a high sign, and *started walking toward each other right out in the open.*

When they got to a point where they couldn't go any farther without smacking each other in the face, they stopped and talked for a few moments, turned, and started heading right back across the open field, north toward us. The entire time my friend and I were staring at each other with the sourest of looks on our faces. Neither of us had seen anything like it in all our days of hunting. Who in their right minds would attempt to drive deer without ever stepping into the natural cover and walking through the place where they actually are? These two simply walked right by the cattails and expected the deer to happily jump out right in front of them.

They hadn't been gone for more than twenty minutes when they returned, the entire time never having left our sight. My friend and I weren't happy, and although he had a few choice words for the pair, Tom said them aloud only to me. (I don't have to enumerate the four-letter words here.)

The pair had plenty to say, though. Apparently, that was one of the few times ever that they had made that "push" and *not* seen any deer. The fervor with which they relayed previous examples was augmented by how incredulous they were about not seeing anything this time. And shot them they had, they told us: does many, many times, as well as several bucks, including a big eight-pointer the previous year. All by walking up the edge of the cattails in a wide-open field! Unlikely as it may be, I found myself believing them without ever having seen proof of their success. How come? The way in which they believed their own story was enough.

A hunter's ego has its rewards. Every story he tells is imbued with the idea that he has somehow bested his "opposition"—that is to say his friends, family, and hunting partners are in competition with him and that he must impart to them his outstanding skills and talent. This can be in the form of how he finds his game or how he makes his way about the woods and fields, his steadfast canter, almost as a horse high-stepping with pride. By verbally imparting this somehow unique and outstanding skill that *only he* possesses, he can then find out how truly skillful he really is *by the reaction of those to whom he tells the story.*

Telling his friends that he came across the biggest buck of

his life had better be followed by rock-hard solid proof, right? But when proof is nonexistent, the hunter's ego is woven inside of great stories. His peers will listen intently to his tales of oak swamps and cover so thick that only deer can penetrate it; their ears will be bent by descriptions of a "record-size rack the size of a truck," and, in turn, they will zero in on size and proportion. They will begin to pry for more specific information about where one can find such a magnificent beast, but the hunter's ego won't give up that information . . . *not yet.* He won't unveil the exact location of the discovery because the details of how he came to find that spot are more alluring. *Like that time he found that swamp full of mallards on that remote side road that nobody knew about, or the story of how he single-handedly came across that vine-ridden old apple orchard where all the grouse were holed up.*

This requires the hunter to be in possession of such basics as an ability to consistently and correctly identify the smaller details: Calling acorns "oak fruit" won't score him any more points than calling a fox a "red coyote." He doesn't just need to know the habits and haunts of his favorite game but why they do the things they do. His own ego demands that he be as proficient with his knowledge of game as he is with his favorite firearm. This includes everything from flora and fauna to wind and water.

We all know the guy who has his fair share of stories about what he *saw.* He is truly the best "eye hunter" out there, and he doesn't mind telling you so. It's that he always seems to misremember the finer, more pertinent details when he comes back empty-handed. Take for instance that time an old friend had been telling me and my group about the Canadian geese that were using a corn lot down by some railroad tracks a couple of towns over: "They looked like a cloud, there were so many of them!" he exclaimed. "You could take one shot and get your limit." So we had to wonder why he never came back with any. It turned out that while the geese were indeed using a cornfield by the hundreds, he failed to mention that the field was part of a wildlife sanctuary on a federally protected wetland.

There is no overt attempt to lie, only to embellish on his adventure. We can forgive and forget the unintentional misrepresentations of a well-meaning friend who only has the desire to add to the group and express his own version of a great hunting story. What is not as easily forgiven is when one of the group has consistently threadbare details and empty hands. We want our friend to be successful because that success reflects upon us as a company. A house needs a good foundation, and the foundation of a good hunting community is based on its individual parts.

And when proof exists, when he has proven his worth in the field over and over by continually bringing back game bags full of game and not stories? Well, we are right there with him, celebrating and patiently listening, time and time again, while he tells us the whole damn story.

The hunter's ego is stroked by a triumphant harvest or fanned in the flames of the reaction he gets from those around him. All hunters have success at some point, but having a trophy without someone to whom to brag about it is meaningless.

OUTDOOR APPRECIATION

Appreciation is the beginning of the sportsman's life, and hunters have a head start on most who would call themselves nature lovers: They've seen the forest from inside its limbs and bows at a time when it was full of snow, when breaking winds jumped them like a mountain lion on a whitetail deer. While most people wouldn't think of walking through freshly fallen snow, hunters sing the songs of the harvest while treading lightly on it. In the spring, they don mud boots while looking for turkey signs in the heart of what will become the sting of bug country in no time. Among the popping ferns and fiddleheads they discover, yet again, that they've been bitten by more mosquitoes and black flies by the end of May than had employees of an entire office building in the busiest city. These cuts, bruises, and bites are the hunters' badges of honor. They've earned them.

Every patch of evergreen or poplar, every low-lying bit of old grapevines and bramble, marks territory calling to be explored. Pushing your face through low and spindly branches as a twig slaps your cheeks is meant to be an awakening—a simple face-crunching indignity that instills in you a vigor that marks the beginning of respect for the outdoors.

But in the dead of summer, when the sun beams through the languid trees and the hunt is only a memory, hunters find other ways to enjoy the outdoors. Picnics are great, sure. We play with the kids and the dog and lounge in the tall ant-filled grass. In the afternoon, we take walks and discover new trails leading to unimaginable peaks. And when we can no longer stand the heat, we seek beaches as refuge.

In our occasional evening solitude, we feel the urge to walk our own yards with our eyes gazing at the stars, to see not only where boundaries lie but to remind ourselves of how small we really are, and how little we know.

We cannot sit still. With our outdoor dreams raging inside of us, we will purchase the hardened steel of our firearms by credit card or go to the shooting range to enjoy the calming outlet of spraying ammunition at air and paper. A camping trip can help; it's a great change of pace for the hunter to get into the woods to observe, with no pressure to harvest. The woods have an irresistible effect on the hunter, who has sated the impulse by being as near to it as he can get without doing it. For another two months, he'll have to pacify his hunger and spend time with the birds, who harmonize his sorrow and, though he may not admit it, are appreciated dearly.

By sitting indoors, he gleans all the adventures he wants to undertake once he actually gets *out there*. He will study, make mental notes, and begin to implement his idea of where he will begin his next outdoor adventure. The hunter has many off-season "workouts" that he uses to not only create his best experience afield but to remind him of the time he enjoys spending outdoors. He may repaint decoys or repair a tree stand. His attention may turn to the simple task of cleaning his firearms or taking stock of his clothes.

He nurses his dreams of the winter hunt over a frosty glass of beer or a long-awaited splash of wine. He will even spend time on the phone with friends and family relating the far-reaching details of the hunt that he loves. He is at once both dreamer and orator of his notions and philosophies. For concepts to take shape and begin to form their way into reality, he must first bounce them off the wall of his own hunting community, which has the effect of both reaping free advice and curating a relationship based on mutual respect.

Sometimes this requires the hunter to imagine future hunts, akin to a baseball player envisioning cracking his next home run.

During these hot summer months, he knows that his quarry inhabits its familiar haunts even without his actually seeing them. His eyes will scour ground and bush until they reveal to him the faint evidence of an animal's movement. Footprints, hoofprints, even obvious marks of bird's feet are proof enough that his senses don't lie. Tracking will bring him to trails on which he'll spot deer prints as numerous as cars streaming on a highway. Without seeing any deer he has, in fact, seen them all.

Envisioning the animal that made this mark—where it came from and where it went—gets his thoughts brewing. Gone from his mind are the green leaves and gratuitous heat, and what survives is the longing to dominate the indomitable. As he tracks the prey in his imagination, the scenery changes from green to white, from perspiration to transmutation. He imagines himself in the freezing cold on a duck hunt, with eyes steady, unblinking.

The uninitiated haven't a clue as to where the mind can take them, having never set up sixty or more decoys in four-foot rollers on any one of the five Great Lakes *in the pitch black*, then waiting to view the sunrise over the eastern horizon. Sitting low in a homemade duck blind—constructed from the squall litter of January—on the shore of a large lake in early winter might not sound like much fun to most; but for the hunter, who has thought about the opportunity for months, it's the epitome of outdoor appreciation. Once his eyes set upon half a dozen mallards coming in from the main lake and looking for a resting place, the cold is no longer part of his consciousness. Once the greenheads and hens have responded to his call, so dies the wind. His hands are no longer frozen and his feet slowly pulse back to life. In an instant, his shotgun loudly reports and he finds himself wading up to his waist in water that has ice floating in it, decoys tethered to the lake bottom and bouncing around him. He thus discovers the reason for hunting during such a foreboding and reckless season: a drake mallard with a creamy emerald headgear lying lifeless upon the water, waiting to rest in the grasp of his yearning hands.

Blue skies and fair weather are the bane of the hunter's existence. In contrast, a steady northeast wind on the lake means the ducks will be flying closer to the shore, or that a big snow the night before an elk hunt means they will stand out and, moreover, be easier to track. The beauty of autumn's changing leaves is one of the hunter's favorite things, but until those leaves drop from the trees, the grouse are hidden and the arrow has less of a target. The grunts of a big swamp gator in September are music to the ears of alligator hunters across the south and the causes of many a barbecue, but pulling one off the bottom when they decide they're going to stay there is like towing a tractor trailer with a bicycle. The hunter can find a strange simplicity and exhilaration in things that make his life more difficult, since he knows they might also show him his greatest victories.

Perhaps it began in the early days, during those car rides he took with his family on a random road that burrowed its way through hills and valleys toward an unknown destination. Back then it was called "taking a ride," but it might as well have been called "getting lost."

The sight of the forest climbing up the hills on both sides of the road was enough for him to imagine deer, turkeys, and grouse behind every tree. Seeing the way those trees stood tall and gripped the landscape he could tell exactly how the hills were shaped and where the peaks and valleys were. He could see it in the way the forest climbed its way toward the sky, and in the way it fell precariously down; how it showed what was obviously the crest of the hill and the way that the trees spilled over the sides. Sometimes those trees looked like soldiers on a march, their orders placed and their destination ahead of them. Other times they looked as if at rest, reconnoitering and ready to bivouac at a moment's notice. Some lucky young men and women would see elk, bear, and moose before those same trees would hide them completely. If he thought he saw something, he had only fallen prey to his imagination.

Even bare trees, maybe *especially* bare trees, have an intense beauty about them. The strength of their limbs is easy to spot, as observed through their naked arms that direct the eyes on and upward. Their cousins in the woodlot, the evergreen trees, sit in patches on their own, lonely islands bursting with green, some sentinels smattered about on the watch. From the window of a moving vehicle, one has the urge to climb them and find what's up there, to look down upon the whole picture.

Shared stories from elders created the dream he took with him into young adulthood, which fostered in him the inspiration for his own adventures. He can remember listening to tales of the Black Hills of South Dakota and of Pike's Peak; of the venerable and stunning state parks around the United States or Canada—places like Arches and Canyonlands National Parks in Utah or the visually stunning Banff National Park in Alberta, or the amazing waterfalls and cliffs of Watkins Glen and Robert H. Treman State Parks in the east, just to name a few. Not only have these attractions become national treasures, they have created a legacy of travel and a roadtrip culture rife with feelings of accomplishment. The hunter's story is founded upon individual discovery, though his soul screams with a desire to show his friends and loved ones what he realizes in all of this: that there is a hunt out there waiting to happen. There will come the time when he'll share this shrewd exploration with others. He'll take his friends back with him on a walk amid shale layers that rise through lichens, brackens, and moss; he'll choose to climb with them on a mountain of ferns and wet stone, careful to not be *too careful*. The hunter understands from the beginning that this world exists for everyone to partake of and use for the good of all, though how we define *good* is often skewered. For no hunter who has plied the fair chase long enough has been without the difficulty of one thing: His love of life is stigmatized by his role in causing death. The hunter doesn't just see the woods; he *is* the woods. He feels the cut when a tree is dropped by a chainsaw, and he aches inside when he walks up to game, bleeding but still very much alive. Even though he understands that death is a natural part of the life cycle, it gives him pause to learn that he is expediting it. He feels for the animal because he is an emotional human, but to be successful he must also harden himself to this reality. The hunter without true feeling for his prey can never really appreciate his world or the hunt itself. This is why so many of us genuflect before the hunt—and, if need be, on the spot as well—for a safe and clean kill, to give thanks to God for all He has provided.

—•—

In North America, it surely began with the Native Americans, who had many gods and were respectful for the nature that sustained them. Consider this: Down at the mouth of some creek they netted and captured lake-run fish, possibly rainbow trout. Above, on the hillside, it must have been easy to stalk deer or ambush other game around the hidden corners of a hollow that the same creek provided. Imagine, if you will, a proud Native American shadowing deer with only a homemade bow and arrow. Consider the shallow water under his feet masking his sound and movement, the walls of the grotto obscuring his presence.

There's no doubt that the beauty of the lakes and creatures wasn't lost on these people. They gave the waters incredible names, like Seneca and Canandaigua, Okeechobee and Huron. They called the hunting wolf *maheegan* and the bear *makwa*. When hunting they saw a spirit in the animals of the earth and meant to keep their souls and purpose alive for all generations to come. They did this by imbuing each animal with characteristics that they hoped to see in themselves. For instance, the badger was seen as a bold communicator and a guardian. Dreaming of one meant that the hunter's persistence would lead him to a victory over his opponent. The bear meant strength, solitude, and a penchant for learning. To dream of the bear was to symbolize life, death, and renewal.

They revered the animals and the sky and the heavens as all hunters do. They told stories from generation to generation about the creatures they hunted and why. They felt that each animal had a kindred spirit in nature and was there to exist with the hunter on the earth that they shared. In Cherokee culture, the tendons and parts of the hamstrings of deer were not to be consumed by any tribal member. When a deer was killed, these particular muscles would be left on the remains as a sign of respect to the spirit of the animal.

In similar fashion, the knowledgeable hunter understands the spiritual meaning of his pursuits—he knows how to look inside and outside of himself to see creatures as more than a conquest. Perhaps the Native Americans didn't expect to learn something beyond where the deer were running or the ducks were flying. But their capacity for understanding the beasts they hunted is noble. Similarly, the concessions to these creatures' needs—a place of respect in our world all their own—is the beginning of truth for us as hunters.

We never cared that oak trees were good for anything other than firewood until we found out that deer love acorns. Who knew what a hedgerow was for, besides those in the farming community, until the first time we flushed a rooster pheasant out of one? Old orchards and grapevines were just lost souls of some long-ago farmers until our hearts exploded the first time a grouse came thundering out of one. It's appreciation that drives us to learn why a deer eats what it eats, but it's determination that makes us study ways to make the herd flourish. For example, I rarely take a doe on opening day, though I'm more than capable of doing so. This decision suggests that we watch those few that aren't hunted yet, those deer that are still green from the summer doldrums. Seeing them act "naturally," pawing at the ground while moving about on well-known trails, gives us a sense that all creatures have taken notice of what they need and are preparing to take advantage of it, much like we do as hunters.

One time I followed the tracks of a ruffed grouse, a bird roughly the size of a small chicken with a similar gait, through the snow. The tracks ran wildly in and out of the cover until they ultimately came to a stop in open hardwoods on the edge of some pines. Here, in hills on the venerable public hunting grounds known as the High Tor Wildlife Management Area, the lay of the land can go from mild to severe in a matter of minutes. One second it can be relatively flat, and the next it can change to an indomitable track of hill, like riding a bull with your feet on the ground.

As I approached the spot where, seemingly, the grouse had stopped, it was clear to see from the feather prints on the snow that this sneaky bird had launched quietly (even the nefarious thunderbird can do just that) and escaped me without my ever hearing or seeing him. Lifelong hunters of these birds will tell you that they get the nickname "thunderbird" for good reason, as their launch from the forest floor or pine bow is akin to a heart attack on wings. Perhaps the thing most appreciated by the ruffed grouse hunter—such was the position I found myself in that day—is the fact that they can escape like no other animal can. Launching and achieving a speed of 1,000 miles per second (no, it's not scientific, but I'm standing by it) is part of their heinous plan to outwit us. Another is how they magnificently duck and weave through trees and coverts to literally dodge our BBs, driving us to continue the chase. My stubbornness in this incident wasn't on account of the bird having outwitted me by way of its usual launch, or weaved its way through the forest, letting my load of seven-and-a-half shot bounce off of some tree; no, it was because it had burrowed *into the snow.* While the ruffed grouse will naturally snow-burrow to avoid enemies like the owl, the goshawk, or even the cold, I had never witnessed this occurrence before. Instead of walking right by it, I had walked right into it.

If only I could relate the utter shock at bending over to more closely observe the spot where this little grouse seemed to have flown away but had gone snowbound, and how, upon further inspection, it shot up just as quickly and escaped through the trees. To this day I can feel the snow hitting my face; I can still hear the sound of the most intense grouse flush of which I have ever been a part. I watched it escape through the woods, turning hard left and then disappearing behind some pine trees, its speed and deftness puzzling me for some time. There can be no doubt then or now: A man with a loaded 12-gauge shotgun is no match for *a missile-powered chicken that can fly.*

What is it about chasing a bird with rocket reflexes, which escapes while continuously laughing at you? Perhaps one of the most commendable parts of the hunter's nature is that he bends but does not break. He has come to grips with the fact that to obtain that which he truly desires—a successful harvest—he must fall on his face a few times. In a never-ending journey through the tangled vines and brambles of life, he cannot dodge the reality that he is, after all, only human. And in the eyes of his fellow mammals, that is something truly unremarkable.

CONSERVATION

Conservationist may be the most overused and misunderstood word in our repertoire. If we hunt to kill, how are we conserving anything? In the eyes of some, the word *hunter* is often interchangeable with *death dealer*, as if hunters are trading on the black carcass market.

But the fact remains that hunters are among the most ardent conservationists and naturalists. The money taxed from outdoorsmen and women, from the buying of gear, licensing, and even firearms and ammunition, contributes wholly to habitat restoration and wildlife law enforcement, as well as to foundations that research and promote development of the principles for wildlife population. We support a continued drive toward hunting-friendly ecostability in North America, and we're influential in the push for wildlife managers to restrict crop damage, curb disease outbreaks, and help in the elimination of invasive species.

Some of the greatest spokespersons of the conservation community have come from the ranks of hunters and outdoor enthusiasts. Aldo Leopold, the enigmatic conservationist and hunter, helped establish wildlife management as a paid professional discipline. John James Audubon was one of the most famous hunting naturalists of his time. Theodore Roosevelt, perhaps America's most astute hunter and conservationist, once said, "In a civilized and cultivated country, wild animals only continue to exist at all when preserved by sportsmen."

Humans have always understood that survival depends on food obtained from the environment in which we live. It took a long time for us to realize that taking all the animals ultimately meant the end of not only hunting, but the humans hunting them! Most people know how close the American bison came to extinction once European hunting methods entered the North American continent, but there were other animals desired by early settlers once they had set down roots in this massive region of the western hemisphere. The venerable beaver, for example, was valuable as a source of fur to help defeat the cold of winter. European eyes looked west to Canada as a source to supplement the fur trade, but it wasn't as simple as setting out traps, which is made to appear so easy on films and TV. In the early 1800s beaver hunters would furiously paddle for miles upriver against the current, only to set their canoes adrift and silently glide back with the flow. This enabled them to sneak up in plain sight on the beaver—which had scarcely seen humans and, in short order, would swim up to the floating hunters out of curiosity and right into easy gunning range. In winter, when the once-flowing rivers froze completely and beavers sought other means of travel, hunters would walk up to an active lodge and begin to crack open its hard wooden shell, built with the sticks and limbs of local trees. When the beaver family panicked and tried to escape, the hunters sought out the *washes* or swimming lanes that went to and from the lodge. This was done by thumping the ice nearest to the bank, then listening for a hollow sound near the escape holes. By now, the hunters had learned to grab live beavers with their bare hands, a small reward for such extreme measures, exacerbated by the severe bite wounds that they surely received.

Remember, this was the order of business in those days. No seasons, no bag limits, and, worse, no rules of engagement. In other words, hunters could walk right up to a lodge full of beavers and break it open, day or night. They shot them from floating canoes or from the riverbanks. They could grab them out of the water and bludgeon them with truncheons. As beaver populations decreased and it was apparent that they were becoming scarce, hunters would move on without remorse or guilt. In our day and age, this would be a fine example of poaching.

But the responsible hunter saw the folly of this plan, and his heart changed course. Eventually, as technological and medical advances increased the rate of survival among Americans, a new ideal emerged in the hunting community: that the hunter dare not take wantonly from his surroundings without restraint lest his surroundings become his eventual grave. Simply put, taking more than the land is capable of sustaining, whether animal or vegetable, is like drinking the last drop in your cup and expecting it to refill itself. Thus seasonal hunting was born, and limits to how many of an animal a hunter could take, and even what sex, were initiated. For the first time, the hunter became the eyes and ears of conservation practices, understanding the habits and the haunts of these much sought-after creatures. Part of the solution came from the wellspring of new wildlife conservation laws and the birth of the esteemed wildlife law enforcement community to oversee not only the creatures that the hunter considers most valuable but the hunter himself.

This is not to say that many in our much needed and highly respected scientific community are hunters, or that nonhunters aren't a big part of the solution as well. Indeed, many are not hunters and never will be. But they respect or at least try to comprehend what the hunter sees, which is the foundational understanding that animals themselves need to hunt for survival, just as humans do. While we no longer need to chase down our lunch or dinner and kill with our bare hands, we recognize that the natural environment is in constant ebb and flow. Predatory animals that overhunt their home range soon begin to disappear from that range, just as animals with few or no natural predators will overpopulate and become too numerous for their surroundings to support.

Since most hunters have a favorite game animal, anything short of trying to conserve that passion for posterity is irresponsible. Perhaps this is why so many hunters get behind—in spirit and in dollars—organizations that support conservation. The hunter wants an animal to thrive so he can have a sustainable population to hunt and never have to consider its demise due to his lack of effort in restoring or revitalizing its numbers.

Organizations such as Pheasants Forever, Rocky Mountain Elk Foundation, Ducks Unlimited, and National Wild Turkey Federation, just to name a few, have large hands in perpetuating the very species to which hunters are most drawn. Even the National Wildlife Federation understands that hunters and fishermen are part of a "core constituency" based on their recognition of core issues that sportsmen value, such as habitat restoration and pure water conservation, not to mention the continuing education of our young people in topics of environmental awareness.

Even the hunter who does not belong to an organization, and never will, has a decided interest in seeing the game of his choice thrive. The common link between those who become a part of these venerable organizations and those who do not is an interest in always seeing wild game when they are afield. It's not only about the creatures that inhabit an area but about that area itself. In the eyes of the hunter, wild land that was once used for farming and has again become fallow is springing with value. Man and his machines may have plowed it, planted it, and reaped its benefit, but now fruit trees and vines have been joined by saplings and grass. Between the cover it creates for the wildlife that now uses it and the food that is still there, man has now reaped another harvest from the conservation of this land: the wild game that inhabits it.

An equally important part of conservation is the decision to react. During a Pheasants Forever seminar back in the 1980s, my friends and I learned that sorghum grass, which doubles as a sweetener in southern states and is useful as livestock feed, is also gluten free and can be made into ethanol. It serves as a fast-growing, drought-resistant plant that pheasants and other game birds use as food. In learning about this plant, we became attuned to what others in our own area were constantly talking about, which, invariably, would become a common phrase in the hunting world: The "food-plot," as it was called, was necessary in easing the strain of wild animals searching for food in the winter. Like detectives in the outstanding game of nature, we adapted this knowledge and specialized in learning how to develop the best possible plots.

When one has decided to set his or her mind to discovery, the results are stunning. Take for instance wild turkey restoration in New York State. New York's Department of Environmental Conservation has estimated that before the Europeans first arrived on these shores the eastern wild turkey, a native of North America, thrived in almost every inch of New York that existed south of the Adirondack Mountains. Then the early settlers began to cut down forests and create small farms, and the turkey was hunted as a food source year-round. By the 1840s, most of the original population of wild turkeys in the Empire State had disappeared.

Within sixty years, the Industrial Revolution had taken hold and farming declined. By the 1940s, some wild turkeys had begun to naturally cross New York's southern border northward from Pennsylvania in an effort to reestablish themselves in territory where they had once thrived. It had been almost a hundred years since turkeys had darkened the doors of New York, and this migration signified their return. Once these birds began to establish solid breeding populations, their numbers rapidly increased.

By 1960, New York had already begun to live-trap turkeys for release in other parts of the state. The first birds were trapped in Allegany State Park in 1959; today, the bird population in New York sits somewhere between 250,000 and 300,000—a feat accomplished by people determined to see a wild animal reestablish its original home range. Hunters and conservation groups were integral to this effort, and neither would allow their hard work to give way to a return to overuse and overharvesting. In 1973 the National Wild Turkey Federation was founded, whose stated mission is "the conservation of the wild turkey and the preservation of our hunting heritage." It was the objective of these men and women to serve as volunteer surrogates in an effort to conserve habitat, procure private lands for hunting opportunities, and both reestablish and secure native wild populations. This same basic mission of ensuring that native wild game populations are healthy and viable for future generations is at the forefront of all "preservation" societies and is spearheaded by the hunting community itself.

Strength in numbers is not only a platitude but a virtue. The uniformity felt within group settings has led me to become a member of Ducks Unlimited, Pheasants Forever, and even Bassmaster, to name a few. It's one thing to tell yourself that you can adhere to the conservationist mind-set on your own, but it won't have the same effect as being held accountable by your peers. In the same ways that we hunt in groups—for advantageous success, camaraderie, and even safety—we conserve in groups too. Even when the hunter finds himself alone in the woods, the objectives set forth by group initiative remind him of his cause.

I taught my son while he was growing up that it was necessary for all individuals to self-regulate, but self-regulation also implies a larger, collective effort. It means that the individual who respects game seasons, bag limits, and such specifics as the taking of a certain sex or age of animal must also be conscious that his fellow hunter tries to do the same. This mind-set of safeguarding the wild outdoors for our future generations sets the hunter apart from those who consider the hunt a useless and self-serving thing.

4

THE WISDOM OF OUR ELDERS

There are two things that interest me: the relation of
people to each other, and the relation of people to land.

—ALDO LEOPOLD

I'm not sure if it was the rooster ring-necked pheasant that I
watched bounce off the windshield of the family grocery-getter as
we drove down those sandy paths toward my grandfather's ranch
in Nebraska's Sand Hills, or the time that my grandfather—
Grandpa J., as we called him—came home one evening with a
brace of prairie chickens ready for my grandmother's kitchen
knife, but it was the visiting and observing of the way that they
lived there that made me fall in love with the idea of hunting and
eating wild game.

As a kid, I never witnessed the actual butchering of those

hens, but once they were set with love on the table in front of Grandpa J. (an old-school man of Lebanese descent), I was entranced by them. The first evening I saw one set on his placemat—adorning his plate with all the grandeur of a meal fit for a king—I hopped into his lap and pleaded for a bite.

His answer? A stern no: the kind a kid with lofty ambitions and a mean appetite never forgets.

In denying me, the lesson he was trying to teach, I learned later, was that to enjoy eating game you must put in your own work to find it and hunt it for yourself, since nothing in the hunting world is a given. To fail and go hungry is tragic, but to not try is an even more heinous thought. How a young boy would have ascertained that lesson (or gone out for the hunt by himself) is lost on me, but my grandfather was not one to simplify anything.

I was ten years old when I went on my first hunt. My uncle took my grandfather deer hunting on his property, and I got permission to tag along. We drove to the back of his land and set up in a bit of cover that separated two fields. Except my uncle did what he always did: parked his club cab dually Dodge pickup with the tubbed-out wheel wells and . . . *sat in the truck's bed*. As certain as I am that my uncle was just making things comfortable for Grandpa J., and that many skilled hunting folks have had the opportunity to shoot a deer from the back of a big bad pickup truck in this manner, my uncle was not one of them. For him, the truck's bed was a comfortable spot that made up for his technical inadequacies. There may not be many places where that style of truck hunting would be legal now, but back then, on his own property, with his elderly father at his side, it was a loving gesture that I recall with fondness.

That day was not the first time I held a gun, but it was the first time I used one on a hunt. The thrill of attending my first hunt accompanied by my grandfather was one-part excitement and two-parts trepidation. He was more than just the patriarch of my family; he embodied everything that we held dear. I didn't want to disappoint him.

Seeing the open stubble of the cornfield on one side and cut beans on the other was espying paradise, but it was nothing compared to the sight of my grandfather sitting next to me in quiet introspection, waiting for the first deer to come forth. I tried to see what he could, but all I managed to ask myself were the nascent questions of inexperience: *Would that big buck I dreamed about show up? How soon? And when it did, would I get to shoot first, or would I have to wait for the adults?*

I imagined the shot and wore out my neck looking back and forth for the deer, because it was sore when I peered back at my uncle and grandfather behind me, who were laughing. I must've looked quite ridiculous preparing for the inevitable target, but look I did, and I've never stopped looking since.

It was my father who taught me how to shoot, plinking with his old single-shot .22 at my cousin's house in the country. Now and then he would bring out his beautiful old break-action single-shot Ithaca 12-gauge and shatter the outdoor silence, pumping birdshot into an old car that we set up with a myriad of bottles and cans. A single dose of his shotgun rang out, and we'd start setting up all the targets again, and it was just as much fun to watch his shotgun mule-kick him as it was to watch him fill that old rust bucket with lead. While my cousins had their own set of rules, enforced by my aunt and uncle, dad's rule to my brother and me was simple: *Don't plug anything that's living. Not yet.*

As such, we had never seen anything so beautiful as an old beat-up Chevy with a million holes in it. My two cousins, Tommy and his older brother, Stevie, would use these old "beaters" as lot cars—something to drive around the old apple orchards—until their engines died on the spot and my cousins deserted them there, turning them into the best shooting target for which one could hope. By the time I got to use the cars for practice, all of the glass, which was the best part to shoot, was smashed and cast off into the dirt in millions of pieces.

My father's understanding of why it was okay to take wild game was based in part on his service as a naval sailor in World War II. As part of the "Greatest Generation," his views on the value of life and death were based on self-reliance. He was born into a household that idealized frugality, that prioritized the idea of DIY before it became a catchphrase, and this morality extended into what he later taught his kids: No way would he take parenting advice from anyone else except what he had learned from his own parents, and so the do-it-yourself mentality was passed on to me and my siblings as it had been to him. If shooting at a car was going to be our first introduction to the hunt, then so be it.

My father would spend much of his time reading articles from each month's *Popular Mechanics* magazine. He made so many things from scratch, taking lessons straight from the pages. He became an expert aluminum welder—not an easy skill— and once built an aluminum outboard motor rack out of scrap from his days working at the venerable Rochester Products. He excelled in everything from building his own boat to making his own fishing lures. He even survived an incident in which his boat capsized, and he had to swim nearly three miles to shore against a stiff southern wind from well out on Lake Ontario. He often spoke of the days when he and his carpool partner would stop on the way in to work when they saw pheasants, shooting them for dinner and leaving them in the trunk for later.

But self-reliance was not always about teaching us how to weld or to shoot in order to perfect skills of survival; it was about learning how to not be afraid to try—to explore the limitless possibilities for which nature stood.

He was instrumental in my outdoor education. Among other things, he and my maternal grandmother taught me to capture my own bait for fishing, putting "wormers" in a coffee can and then in a homemade plywood crate full of leaves and other fancy mulch that included grass clippings. As a young boy, schooled in the fine art of crawling on my hands and knees, sometimes in the rain and always at night, I was a voracious sponge in the game of bait gathering. I caught night crawlers by the thousands. Even before that, I have early memories of Grandpa J. teaching me how to catch grasshoppers for the hook. Watching him use his hands—with its calluses and busted knuckles—while crawling around on his knees in a pair of well-used coveralls taught me lessons in dexterity and patience. It looked funny at first, but to this day I still use the same method for frog hunting: I wait until they settle down, get my hands way out in front of them, and then slowly close in the same direction until they hop right into my waiting little paws—*or don't*. For people like my father and grandfather, stalking and preying and intimidating was as important as the capture itself. You were either better than nature, or you were owned by it.

To them, a grasshopper in the hand meant a future fish on the hook. They taught by example, first crawling through the thick tangle of tall grass surrounding the water, then trying their own luck with the fishing rig. They could hook bait on their fishing lines, throw them in the pond, and reel in a catch within minutes. Over and over they repeated this pattern until there was enough for everyone to have not only lunch but dinner as well. These were the good times, when watching them felt akin to doing it myself. Until I had to do it myself. Once it was time for me to get down and dirty, to crawl around in the tall grass and catch my own grasshoppers for bait, the spring-tailed bugs with the ability to fly would wait until the last second, almost teasing my fingers, and then launch to the next tall blade of grass to start the game anew. To fail was one thing, but to quit was unacceptable. My grandfather made me aware of this. He knew that a child would have a hard time doing what he proposed, but that didn't matter to him. Consider the beginning of this chapter once again, in which I was denied that tasty, fried wild bird. In denying me the occasional treat, he made it known that I had not helped in the hunting nor the cleaning of this hard-earned meal. I had not milked the cows, nor fed the pigs, nor brought in the pails of milk to the cream separator (did I even know what a cream separator was?). I had not captured the grasshoppers.

While those broad-shouldered men in my life taught me the hard lessons (such as what happens to you when you leave the worm box in the sun), it was my mother, Lucille, who instilled in me kindness. The eldest of eight children growing up in Nebraska, she knew how to raise a child before she ever had any of her own. Don't get me wrong: She was also tough as nails, and she had an occasional wrath that only a girl growing up twenty-five miles from the nearest town, and in the 1930s, could have. For her, hunting meant taking care of her young siblings in a way that protected them from harm. She grew up where rattlesnakes, bull snakes, garter snakes, and water snakes were known to thrive, and she was taught that these reptiles had the undisputed right of way. The Nebraska summers were hot and dry, and many of these snakes would seek out the water sources that a farm always possessed. She frequently told stories of being a young girl and standing near the stock tanks or any other water puddle, and seeing and hearing snakes by her feet. She'd call the adults, and soon enough she would find that snake hanging over a wire fence without its head, like a precursor to the hunting trophy, one that no taxidermist could mount better.

This didn't mean that my mother had some great urge to kill, only that she knew it was a necessary part of living in the rough environment that was her home. She lived as she was taught: to respect the lives of all animals while understanding that some of them were threats.

The provocation of violence by them, to her, was a simple but effective reminder.

The hunt is the fountain of youth of the outdoorsman; the well-spring by which he lives. Take away that which he sees as his indomitable right, and you withdraw his usefulness. He needs to know that, even in his old age, he can go forth and pursue; that it will always be there waiting for him.

The same held true for my grandfather during that hunt when he brought me into the fold for the very first time. In that moment, he was a man of the truest grit with an unending determination, but as his unfiltered smokes and the marching of time would tell, his legs could carry him only a little more than his eyes could see. He was in his seventies and had the will of a badger, but his bite lacked the steel it once held. He could still carry his firearm and could easily have shot it, but on this day, we would hear only the report of other hunters in the woods. After every shot in the distance I dreamed of deer crossing the open field; every time that I looked at him to see his reaction, I saw the dormant hunter in him waiting to uncoil.

Eventually, the physical place he took in the hunter's hierarchy was surpassed only by the edification that he left me, a wisdom we seek for not just redemption, but as a path to absolution. As my grandmother Alice always said in her blessing before every meal: "Bless this food, O Lord, for the use of our bodies."

Give me six hours to chop down a tree and I will spend the first four sharpening the axe.

—ABRAHAM LINCOLN

Part Two

THE PREPARATION

5

THE HUNTER AS DETECTIVE

If the woods are nature's theater, trees are their loving and playful props. Hunters move around them over the course of a season and come to learn them as they would idiosyncrasies of their own home:

> That one over there with the strange burl.
> The oak with the gnarly knot in it.
> The maple where we set up our stands last time.

We learn to gumshoe, relying on our ears before our legs are ever needed. We seek word-of-mouth information, much like how fishermen trying out new lakes need to know where the fish are biting. As important as it is to ply friends and acquaintances for intel and relate to their exploits afield, it is just as important to listen. Hunters tell memorable stories when given the opportunity; they want to boast about their successes in a way that defines their roles in the pecking order but also grants their fellow hunters similar opportunities. This is how I first learned of such things as the incomparable shotgun choke-tube: the simple but effective device that allows the spraying of birdshot in different patterns depending on the type of game, the pattern of "shot" desired, and distance to the target.

But it's not about listening and blindly following. One needs scrutiny—the ferry boat the hunter rides that narrows the gap between refining awareness and future success.

I found out many years ago that if I set my decoys out too early in cold winter conditions they would be completely frozen over before first light, making them less than satisfactory as a counterfeit group of mock waterfowl. The hunter continuously searches for the ways that use the least amount of ammunition possible. Not because he is concerned with wasting ammo, but because he is preoccupied with creating the best opportunity before any shot is ever taken: Get them in close from the beginning and odds are that they will go home with you.

The luxury of the hunt without the shot is satisfying in so many ways and serves to dispose the ignominy of the kill. The hunter isn't ashamed or somehow mortified by the taking of his prize—the very opposite is true—but the lack begets another pleasure that's always present but seldom acknowledged. Without a shot to take, there's none to miss. There's no need to adjust the angle or play the wind, nor to assume that every fatal flaw in our well-laid plan will fail us.

———•———

In my younger years, I hunted both the very remote and what I call the "farm deer" nearer to my home. These areas are nothing compared to the mountainous region of the Catskills or Adirondacks, but the peaks and valleys in New York's Southern Tier can be daunting to hunt, to say the least, with their extreme steep angles to walk and the sometimes precipitous cliffs that can catch the hunter completely by surprise. Since all decent hunters—myself included—can be blind to their quarry while they are entranced by the beauty of the surrounding vistas that wind before them, it's here where I had to train myself to stop looking and to start *seeing*. What I mean is that it's easy for the hunter to get lost in this striking place and forget why he came there in the first place. Seeing was made possible by repeat efforts in these impressive landscapes, so that once I had memorized the particulars I wasn't prone to being utterly enveloped by them. I became consciously, blissfully aware of the areas around me, of what was natural and what was not. On the one hand, the forest seemed clean and undisturbed, in a way that had the look of never having been traversed. On the other, it was obvious that men and their machines had noticed something long before I had ever come.

The two experiences can coexist. For one thing, numerous Wildlife Management Areas (WMA) have logging trails created over the course of many years by private landowners and locals with an eye toward cash-crop timber or firewood. While many of these trails have long since overgrown and become reclaimed by the forest, they still offer open, man-made lanes that are useful to wildlife. In more recent years, these areas have been logged to promote the growth of young forest, supplying even more open paths. When walking these hills, it is easy to see how foreboding the habitat is. It has the look of a forested area that has had little to do with the hunter or anyone else for many long years. Some of the trees are incredibly tall and lean and they tilt forward, suggesting a timeless period when the Iroquois roamed this state. Did the Iroquois too get caught up in the beauty to the point of missing their game? Or did their skills and need for sustenance outlast their hunter's easily distracted natures?

While I primarily hunted for ruffed grouse in these WMAs, I also saw a lot of whitetail deer, whose establishment in this area has made them among the most inaccessible and nimble of their species. Their lives are spent moving up and down the rugged hills, to and from the valleys where they can find fields of grain, old orchards, and water. A first sighting means the flick of a tail, or a glint of brown through the snow-covered trees, some kind of motion before it disappears. But it also means being on guard for the unique: an old overgrown hunting cabin swallowed by the forest where the animals would try to bed down and hide, or the edge of a ravine so massively steep that even the deer couldn't scramble away down it and would have to backtrack right by us. Following the trails of deer isn't always the order of business when on a grouse hunt, but I would consistently come across them again and again, considering all the time where I would later set up during deer season and why. One thing that was clear to me at that time was how, when the deer came up or down the hill and onto one of these old logging trails, they would follow it like we would. In other words, the deer want to utilize an easy route, just like you and me. They can slow down and loaf for a while, or browse the brush on the edges for leftover buds. The browse line is easy to see: Everything from the deer's reach down is trimmed like a hedge in summer. And so the deer's ease of escape rivals our ease of passage.

Veteran hunters of this spectacular region know where to set up and, more important, how to stay still. After watching these deer for years on end, hunters recognize the obvious signs of them having been there recently—freshly beaten down mud, or bounding tracks in the snow—but, still, there will be no *sight of* them. High Tor WMA is some 6,800 acres of rugged terrain for the uninitiated, and yet in spring and summer it offers some of the most spectacular vistas and trails that anyone could hope to hike. Deer use this area with impunity and leave calling cards of their obvious passing. With this knowledge in hand, the hunter can deduce the most trail-appropriate area in which to set his stand; with his experience, he knows that the slightest movement will give him away to these ultra-wary deer. And all without ever taking the first shot.

———— · ————

Nearer to home, and north toward Lake Ontario, the land eases into a flatter, more placid landscape—the lake plains as it is known. Here you can find corn- and beanfields just up the road from apple and peach orchards. There is plenty of food available for the venerable whitetail, but make no mistake, in among the varying types of landscape here, there can be areas swampy and thick as well. It's a difficult place to traverse if you're not walking on four hooves, but it's not all this way; there is also farmland in between, edges where deer escape into oblivion or eat at their leisure. Here their trails are obvious as they scrabble in and out of the cover, even in this thick Amazon of the northeast. Here they have no need to climb the mountain and escape; instead they find a respite of cover so thick that nothing can penetrate it . . . or so they think.

The deer are different in these vicinities from their cousins of the hills farther south. Since there are many open spaces where they can be more easily seen, they are used to more interactions with humans. They can be seen in the mornings and evenings gathering in nearby parks and ball fields next to crops, places to reap a mouthful of grass or leftover corn; they even sidestep the farmer as he works his fields. At play, they will kick and swat each other, even rear up and spar. Should the wind come up, they are much more skittish: Their ears will turn and dip on their heads like a radar dish scanning for informational noise and their eyes become roaming motion detectors, but it's their sense of smell that kicks into overdrive. These farmland deer will run just ahead of the hunter, waiting to test the extent of his actions. When the pressure is on they will stand still and let him walk right on by. Deer that think the hunter doesn't see them won't budge. Who will flinch and move first? Wild animals have developed many courageous survival skills, but nonpredatory creatures usually don't count patience among them. They won't stand and wait too long to see whether or not the hunter, or anything else, will storm after them with bullet, arrow, or claw.

The same is true for grouse and especially rabbits. I learned long ago that grouse will wait to flush until after I've walked right by them, starting me down the road of the "take five steps, stop and wait" method. This has the effect of making the grouse nervous or, as I like to say, "crazy." Then, like the deer, they will take off, but at a time of *your* choosing and hopefully not theirs.

For the uninitiated, this is like sitting on the street corner and people watching. You can see the hurried gait of the man who is late for work but had to stop for coffee. If you wanted to intercept him one morning, it would be easy to stake out the shop and wait. Now the question is: When will he be there? Does he go to this same shop each day? What is his favorite drink? Does he ever meet someone there? Why do these things matter? In the woods, the patterned movements of animals reveal characteristics of their behavior linked to things like mating season, hunger, and communal rituals like seeking water. Watching these patterns unfold is an integral part of how each hunter can start down his own road to success (or, at the very least, find the best price for a coffee in his neighborhood).

———•———

The ring-necked pheasant is not native to North America. Ornamental and colorful birds, they were brought to the western U.S. shores from China around 1881 to be established as game birds in Oregon by one Owen Nickerson Denny. Due to their fast-moving, explosive flushes (and their outstanding colors), they have found their way into the hearts of hunting sportsmen for over one hundred years.

The rooster, or male of the species, has a vivid red face and is adorned with an iridescent copper-gold plumage and a confident white collar around its neck, denoting the name. It can be a master of escape and deceit, a ghost of opportunities lost. Whenever its wild cackle emanates from the depth of a hedgerow or from a goldenrod field, our ears flick on and our eyes begin to scan. We consider the hunts of our ancestors, when dogs ran the tall grass to get in an upwind position of these birds.

I look to my own dog.

After some twenty years in the masonry trade (although when it was all said and done, the final count would be thirty-three), I was fortunate enough to build my own home for the first time in the beginning of 2002. It was set on the very last lot at the end of a dead-end street that backed up to old forsaken farmland that the building company had purchased and would eventually become more homes. In the years that I lived there I saw fox, coyote, deer, and a hell of a lot of wild pheasants, including hens that would walk into the yard with a dozen chicks in the spring. There was even a pond in the back on which I would set up for mallards, or just sneak up and jump-shoot them for dinner. At that time, I was three years into full-time gundog training with my German shorthaired pointer, Chase, whom I had gotten as a six-week-old pup. Don't let the masculine name fool you, though, because she was as loving a girl as I could ever have hoped for in a hunting partner.

And as I told my friends ad infinitum: She was hell on birds.

Chase taught me lessons I will take with me for the rest of my life, the most important being trust. It was always my habit to listen for these zany, wild birds behind my home and stalk them by following their sounds. I would try to get Chase zigzagging, with her nose into the wind near where I had last heard the call, hoping she would lock up on point. As it was, this method did work now and again, but there were areas that she always wanted to pursue that I felt were no sense hunting, and I would call her off. One of these spots was right on the edge of the goldenrod field where it met some hardwoods, along the edge of which grew a strange variety of bush: a short tree that had many arms and was replete with these odd-looking white berries that looked as if they would be poisonous to anything that ate them. While I had seen pheasants in the woods before, I had never shot one there.

It was Chase's instinct that took us there over and over. One day, I was smart enough to follow her primal urge to stay and find something. She would disappear in and out of the woods, back and forth between the cover of the tall goldenrods and the thick, berry-laden bushes on the edge. It certainly wasn't the first time I had seen her lock up on point like she did just then, but here it was different. This wasn't the edge of a hedgerow near the stubble of a cornfield. This was an area that I probably would never have tried if not for a four-legged wonder with a spectacular nose.

When the rooster eventually did launch into the air, it didn't get far since I was more than ready to plug it with a number-four load of birdshot. Chase was well trained to hold tight for both the flush and the shot, so she didn't budge until I released her for the retrieve. She was soon at my side with a face full of pheasant, but that success wasn't my concern. I wanted to see what the bird had inside of its crop, and I shouldn't have been surprised: It was full of those same funky white berries! (Not only that, but there were also grasshoppers and a weird yellow beetle with black spots that I had never seen before.)

Over the years I've ascertained how many times Chase was locked on point when there seemed to be no bird there. Yet the scent of the bird is always ripe. Without noticing the back-and-forth movement at the blade-tips of the high grasses, the hunter might think that nothing was there. Imagine watching someone run the slalom on a ski hill, only the hill has a thousand tall poles and there's only one unseen skier. Your eyes will tell you the obvious: There is something moving through the forest—concealed and shifting—trying quickly to escape. This had the effect of fooling even my mighty shorthair, who would stick like glue to the lasting scent and hold her point. I would walk ahead of her ten, twenty, even thirty yards only to release her to come up again. She would immediately find the newest fresh scent left by the scampering bird and lock, only to watch her hunting partner walk ahead for nothing. After suffering through this more than once over time, and losing the bird in every instance,

I drove them toward the edges of the area where the cover ended, causing them to expose themselves one way or the other. One thing I was sure of were the words spoken to me by the woman I hired to teach me to train my girl: "They never make mistakes, they were only taught wrong."

———•———

As far as waterfowl go, I've taken, or have been a part of taking, most every puddle duck and diving duck that there is in the Atlantic flyway. I've taken home goldeneye, bufflehead, mergs (mergansers), hooded mergs, one or two ring-necked ducks (not to be confused with the pheasant), and a lot of bluebills. I've been a part of jump-shooting Canadian geese on ponds and in cornfields, and I've even taken a few brant home from the lakeshore back in the day.

Finding and utilizing a good duck-hunting spot can be work for the ardent waterfowl hunter, and sometimes it comes with a price. I can reminisce about the end of my high school days, when a good car meant driving a beat-up 1969 Dodge Dart. Stop for a moment and text your auto-shop-loving, gear-headed buddy to see if he can remember the old slant-six motor that couldn't be killed with a Thompson submachine gun. This is what I drove around exploring for open swamps, hidden cattails, and bulrushes that must be hiding thousands of ducks. One time, way back in the early 1980s, my friend Kevin and I drove north to my family's cottage in the Cape Vincent area of New York to try our luck at finding the Holy Grail of duck hunting, though, like the Knights of the Round Table, we had no idea where to start. We had never hunted the area in October and didn't have a clue as to where to set up.

When it came time to actually get my decoys, shotgun, and chest waders out of the trunk of that car—which I swear would fit a queen-sized bed—we had found ourselves on a lonely stretch of road bordered on one side by red-bush and scrub brush, and on the other side by cattails and bulrushes that extended out onto a soft, inviting swampy area full of lily pads. It was near an open part of Lake Ontario just before it flows into the St. Lawrence River. There was nothing in sight but empty scrub country backland that amounted to nothing but unused territory by some forgotten farmer. There were no warning signs against trespassers nor obvious places where anyone else had ever used this spot. Only one lonely house up the road could be seen from the road, and even that looked abandoned.

Most of the time it stands to reason that a hunter scouring and storing his information is the foremost way to get the best future result. For two eighteen-year-olds with barely a weekend off from school, it was our prerogative to shoot first and ask questions later. We did just that, and that afternoon we walked out of that isolated and fairly inaccessible swamp with some birds and a desire to come back the next day. Upon returning to the car, I immediately realized that the rear driver's-side tire was almost completely flat and needed a quick change. I threw the flat into the trunk and off we went to find some food and a shop that could plug the tire and replace it as the spare. The kindly gentleman who did the repair brought the recently fixed tire back to us, then proceeded to look us both over with a fine-toothed comb, first my friend and then me. The problem, it seems, stemmed from a hole in the tire in a very odd and unpredictable area, the sidewall. Running over something and causing a flat is one thing, but a patch needed in the side of the tire denotes something else altogether: damage due to a purposeful act.

After a decent night's sleep, we again found ourselves on the same lonely road, sitting in the same off-lake swamp trying to find the mother lode of all duck hunting. As it was, the action was nothing compared to the day before, so we packed things up earlier than usual. We had been hearing some activity out along the road but thought nothing of it at the time, as we were in the process of imagining ourselves the two best duck hunters on earth.

Come to find out, as we walked out of the cover of the bulrushes and looked to the road where my old beat-up rolling rust bucket was parked, someone in their infinite wisdom had taken it upon themselves to park a ten-wheel dump truck up to and touching my front bumper, and an old pickup truck touching my back, making it obvious that someone had decided that we weren't going anywhere. Other than the two vehicles touching both bumpers of my old Dodge, there was no sign of anyone else around. It was clear that there wasn't a place to go except for the lone house at the end of the road.

It seems that this one little bit of swamp, bulrushes, and lily pads was owned by one very old, bedraggled, and seriously pissed-off retired farmer who lived in this house. After berating us for well over a minute, he told us that we could've knocked on his door to ask permission to hunt on his property (not that he would've given it). He admitted that it was he who had stuck a screwdriver into the tire's sidewall the day before, and how he was incredulous when we drove off—how he thought he would never see those two dumb kids ever again because nobody could be that stupid to show up a second time after finding a screwdriver hole in their tire. I thought back to the reaction of the tire repairman, and how we should've known something was up by the way he had peered at us.

After that encounter, we never stopped asking people for permission to hunt. In fact, we asked when we shouldn't have, interrupting people as they were eating a family dinner or walking their dogs. After all, the hunter is bound by his moral obligation to the world that he takes from. Should he happily gain access to his hunt by dedication to an honest method of discovery, he has and always will be granted a lifetime of realization that his process is well mannered and has the greatest chance of success. But should he cut corners, he will find out that what he wants will be like a screwdriver in the sidewall of life: a shortcoming made devastatingly clear.

PRACTICE AS A PURPOSE

I have often thought about the word *practice*, as both noun and verb, on long, solitary walks in the woods. Is there a difference between practicing something and the practice *of* something? Perhaps it's the latter that sounds more serious, and which makes me think about the word *study*, as in the study of classical music or archery; the synergy felt in looking through a telescope as one would peer through a rifle scope. Is the practice of hunting akin to a lifetime endeavor, a philosophy and skill sharpened and refined over time? Is *practicing* simply the pathway to *a practice*? These progressions occupy me as I'm steadying the gun, aiming for the shot, firing, and—always the fool—missing. And then the thought: I may not have *practiced* enough.

When hunters practice, we don't just set up targets and start shooting; we pretend as though we're gearing up for the hunt.

Though we might place a bull's-eye—or, better yet, a full body target—we try to imagine the actual hunt right on the spot. A paper target on a tree fifty yards away might as well be a deer, pheasant, or duck. A popping clay target is a grouse or pheasant about to be clamped in the jaws of a retriever.

After a couple of rounds, during which the drills lose their novelty and the challenge decreases, we move the target farther away or launch multiple clay targets at once. We think ourselves clever, as if alternating the difficulty of a video game. But one thing we can never do is mimic the actual event: The sudden, unsteady, and unpredictable flush of a rooster or grouse out of the thickest cover or a deer's sprint for a thicket is impossible to replicate. In the latter example, replication is indeed frowned upon by some in the hunting community. According to these folks, the practice of shooting at a running deer is an exercise in futility or, worse, a poor choice by a poor hunter. This is because, when it comes to execution, the "escaping" shot is an arrogant attempt to hit a fleeing animal with a very low prospect of doing it well enough to stop it there. Too many times animals have been wounded while escaping, and they don't recover. No hunter wants this; the clean shot, which is the primary goal of every hunter, seldom happens. Even in the best-case scenarios—the motionless animal or straightaway shot at the bird—the hunter will find himself in the uncomfortable position of having too much time or too easy a shot.

Part of practice is *not* taking a shot, even when it appears to be a clear one; it means staying your hand when all your impulses tell you otherwise. I can remember more than one time in my life getting a great look at a deer or a flushing bird, only to see the bright colors of a friend somewhere along the target path. Case in point. Years ago my friend Kevin and I were taking separate paths around a small cattail marsh between two seldom used fruit orchards. He took the low side around the edge of a pine row, and I had the higher ground looking down toward the water. Everything came together perfectly when a bedded eight-point buck detected his presence, rose up off the ground, and tried to let him walk right by. By the time I realized what was happening, raised my shotgun, and placed the crosshairs on his shoulder, I could see my friend's blaze-orange through the trees. Though my hunting partner was at a ninety-degree angle to the right of the deer, he was still in my line of sight. It is, to this day, the hardest shot I *never* took.

I have been fortunate enough to hunt with many different friends over the years, and I have found that each of them has unique views on how to gain that overall success when afield. One group with whom I hunted, a pair of brothers named Tim and Paul, whose parents had property adjacent to some unused woods owned by the local university, would set up to shoot clay pigeons in their backyard. We basically had a private shooting range and could blast away at will. We still found ourselves seeking more of a challenge when it came to popping these aerial targets, so we began to . . . *stop looking at them.*

Here's what I mean: We began to turn our backs to the forest, toward where the flying targets were headed, while still being able to clearly see whomever was acting as the thrower. We would nod and say, "Pull!" Then we'd have to wheel around, pick up the moving target quickly, aim, and fire. While we probably weren't the first to think of this method—and I leave it to the instructor community to decide on its merits and safety—it was the best way we could think of to simulate the way that the mind reacts to the abrupt and unexpected flurry of a bird that flushes when the hunter least expects it, and how to set eyes on it at the same time.

Practice can involve much simpler and more palpable methods, and sometimes they are self-evident. As I said, I take no credit for some of these ideas, but I have found a few things over the years that just seemed obvious, however unconventional, and trying them has paid off for me. In 1993, I was still using a smoothbore 12-gauge shotgun with simple open sights with which to hunt deer. It dawned on me around that time that I should start practicing with both hands. In other words, the right-hander in me took to shooting left-handed in earnest. I remember having no good place to set up a target, so I drove down to the shore of Lake Ontario to a spot where we were allowed to hunt duck. I nailed a piece of scrap plywood to a gnarly chunk of driftwood that was high enough off the ground to suit me and began to shoot lefty. It's as easy a switch as a hunter can make, but would it work in the real hunt? As I found out on opening day that very same year, the answer was a resounding *yes*. At first light, I immediately saw movement on my far right, which is a near-impossible shot for a right-hander unless he can stand up and move his body around—*or turn the firearm in his hands and shoot left-handed*. Since I was tethered in a seated position to a small permanent tree stand, I chose the latter. I shot all five shells that I had loaded, and I hit that deer four times. That buck had started out forty yards away and died touching the tree in which I was posted. Good practice creates good luck.

One of the things that the hunter loves the most is the practice of scouting. It starts by reading the area and then selecting the most appropriate location for a stand. Once a spot is chosen, the hunter will turn around and look at it from a different angle, by which I mean he tries to see what the deer sees; it's the point of view that can make or break him. What has he missed? What can the animal see from this vantage point that might cause it to cut and run before the hunter is ready? There's no such thing as a perfect spot, and at some point, as occurs in any practice, the hunter must let go and begin to trust his ability. He suddenly sees himself in the tree looking down, imagining his quarry dropping on the spot.

The visceral reality of the hunt is not far off now, but that does not mean the work is done. One difficulty that all hunters face, even the tried-and-true veterans of many long hunts, is the issue of holding it together as the shot presents itself. It doesn't matter if one's gator hunting in Florida or trying to put the right pin on a bighorn sheep in Oregon—the latter example allows only one shot before it's gone in a flash—the hunter must be a slave to his own body, aware of its every response. The first order of business is an easy one: to breathe. I learned long ago that as I got excited, I would stop breathing, which would disturb the equilibrium that my body craves. I'd tell myself to breathe, even if that meant making my mouth sound like a humidifier.

For bowhunters at full draw, improper breathing affects the muscles, which require oxygen. They begin to shake, and upon recognition of this weakness, the focus becomes lost. The hunter must imagine the breath in his lungs slowing to try and keep his heart from racing. If he does this in time, he can finally consider his eyes. His emphasis has been on breathing, but now his concentration returns to his sight. With his prey fully in his vision, he can now achieve the deliberate and unceasing awareness of his eyes: the last piece of the puzzle.

When it comes to birding, the routine for controlling one's breath leads to proper emphasis on vision. I wish I could count the times that I blistered the tail feathers on a crossing bird because I didn't breathe enough and, as such, didn't lead my shot. Shooting clay pigeons for target practice can be deceiving at times because the hunter can and will hit the clay, which will lead him to believe that it was a kill shot when it was not. I discovered a practice drill one day, brought on by my desire to have some fun with my kid and the dog. We would get out multiple toys, such as the football, soccer ball, and the Frisbee, partly because my dog, a German shorthair, is as high energy as they get. (German short-hairs are slaves to their will and want to run until they drop.) We would throw one ball one way, a second another, in an attempt to defeat her utter speed and her inspiring desire to get there first. At one point my son tried to throw the Frisbee but managed only a flat, across-the-bow launch that went right in front of me. Since I had the football, I tried to hit it as it crossed my path and discovered immediately that I was woefully behind it. I tried again, and again.

After enough attempts at trying to predict the physics of two intersecting objects, you eventually will hit it. The lesson of trying is tantamount to a slow-motion version of wing shooting: frustrating but eventually rewarding. The same goes for a difficult crossing shot on a bird, particularly something small like a grouse, bufflehead, or teal. Leading and swinging through the shot are vital to success when pass shooting—and one of the toughest yet most fun things for which to prepare. With a prime shot load escaping from the barrel at a rate of some 1,500 or 1,600 fps—yes, that's *feet per second*—plus the different choke tubes available today that deliver shot in distinctive patterns, you would think that the hunter could never miss. It's uncanny that a Frisbee so well reminded me that we can in fact miss. The legendary Davy Crockett was said to have become a great sharpshooter by shooting at things like shot glasses. There's a story that he could shoot the flame out of a candle at fifty yards, reload, and do it again.

Quick decisions often need to be made by the hunter, but they mustn't be made rashly. Again, we are confronted with language that seems synonymous but seldom is: An experienced hunter will tell you that quickly firing off a shot is not the same as firing it off rashly. The older, experienced hunter, who has learned to compose himself in the face of tantalizing impulses, relies upon his methods of practice to appreciate the glory that comes with waiting for the best shot. But even he will have his destiny pulsing in the palm of his hand when it comes time to shoot, an ever-present reminder that the hunt can be controlled, sometimes conquered, but never mastered.

HOW NATURE HUNTS

Ask the animals, and they will teach you, or the birds
in the sky, and they will tell you; or speak to the earth,
and it will teach you, or let the fish in the sea inform
you.

—JOB 12:7–8

At my home in the rural Dickensian village in which I grew up,
we never locked the doors or got nervous upon strangers' foot-
steps approaching our house. When the stars emerged at night,
the talk flowing from under the porch roof died to a hum, and we
would stare into the ephemeral darkness and watch the animals
come out.

Skunks wandered in and out of sight and dug through the
yard, hunting grubs. Their scents scourged our noses, but they

soon became as familiar as our pets'. Cottontail rabbits were and still are a part of any mowed lawn, but the keyed-up opossums that shape-shifted in the distance held industrious, unbreaking stares that gave me chills. The only thrill that could break them was the sight of the red fox or the ghostlike whitetail deer that would grace us, then just as quickly fade from sight.

These disappearing acts became part of larger stories my parents told me, which, as it turned out, were not idyllic tales of creatures with human characteristics, such as what the nonhunting peoples of today's world often try to give them. Instead, I learned that everything lives and dies in various extreme ways, and that their hunting, as opposed to ours, was an absolute necessity.

Nature doesn't need a license. It operates day and night, unrelenting and without remorse. And most of the time the hunts occur "offscreen"—by which I mean far from the cameras of cable's favorite nature shows—and in the deeply worn patches of unseen woods.

Some hunters are lucky, if you can call it that, to spot this chain of command in the wild. My cousin Glen—rest in peace—was the first to tell me a story about losing his catch to another hunter, in his case a snapping turtle. He was fishing in one of the many quarry ponds along the Erie Canal and had hooked something to his metal stringer. "This bass," he said, his hands animating large, sweeping movements, "could fit both of my fists inside of its mouth, with room for more." He recalled peeking over the side of the canoe to view his eminent prize, only to discover that the head and gills were all that were left of this brute of a large-mouth. When it came time to tell me about the snapping turtle that had caused this, he became wistful, if not a little frustrated. "The size of a manhole cover," he said, likely embellishing a bit, but it was a point well taken: One hunter had put a fish on the stringer so another could have it for lunch.

States like Mississippi, Louisiana, and Alabama regularly have "crawfish" boils that are much better eaten than described by me here. But in Missouri, the locals catching crayfish for bait outnumber those using them as a tasty meal; the use of these pincer-endowed crustaceans to catch another hunter is common practice for anyone fishing the famed Table Rock Lake in the Show Me State. As creatures of habit, fishermen here know that some of the best "hunting" begins with a wire-mesh trap and a can of dog food with which to bait it. This hopeless concoction of Alpo and mesh unites man and crustacean in a partnership that can end in a full stringer although, more often than not, catch and release. Once this mess is applied inside the trap and sub-merged, crawdads everywhere will find it and clamber their way into a cell and accept their last reckoning. Big, thick-lipped small-mouth bass, whose daily routine is to hunt down and eat as many of these crustaceans as they can, are the reason these diminutive freshwater "lobsters" are hunted and used to tempt gamey black bass. They are why fishermen revert to their hunting instincts, for when these crawdads are strategically placed on a hook they will lure fish, inviting a strike by way of unmitigated opportunity.

If animals are merely surviving by way of their nimbleness and instinct, humans are effectively plodding, moving along in daft ways. Beyond trusting our senses, we take time to reason, scout, and plan. We reconnoiter areas like marines, looking for the best possible spot to set up, trusting that it will lead us to our kill. Yet animals hunt without knowing if they're going to be successful or go hungry. Some find a host in which to live and some an ambush point from which to attack. Others may use the ground-and-pound method to chase down their prey. If, in following animals' leads, we plunge in haphazardly, thinking the "bum-rush" methods that animals use have their advantages, we'll fail. When a school of tuna attack a mass of sardines there's magic in their chaos, but when we think we can unabashedly make a frontal assault we had better come out lucky.

And why not? Luck is part of the process after all.

A few years back, I happened upon a scene that I might have not believed had I not witnessed it. I started the day on a grouse hunt in Livingston County, New York. After releasing my dog Chase to start her run into the low, lush cover of a thick pine stand brimming with green, I came upon the carcass of a little four-point buck. It had come to rest, still wrapped inside the pine row, lying on the leftover needles, just on the edge of the outer cover that opened out into bramble and thorn apple. As I approached the body of this hopeless wreck, I immediately noticed that Chase had stopped to stare at the spectacle of chickadees working the carcass. On an official hunt, my shorthair was usually relentless, but this was her twelfth year and her attitude was now that of a thinker more than a runner. We stood side by side in awe as dozens of these courageous little fuzzy birds landed, pecked, scattered, and came back for more.

There are no bugs in February, nor are there flowers and seed. For birds in the wild and fallow fields to survive they must thrive on what nature gives them. Watching those birds peck away at leftover bone and sinew left me feeling stark and exposed. These little birds—the most fearless in the woods—have a way of quietly taking on anything on their own, but I soon realized that it was the forlorn little buck that had crushed me. What had killed it: man or beast? I scanned for answers. While there were obvious signs that coyotes had eaten some portion of it, there was still enough left to encourage my inner call for a solution. We can look at it scientifically or sentimentally, but when nature hunts there is not always a fond explanation.

The cruel ways in which the animal kingdom hunts never cease to surprise even the most refined of us. There are documented cases of chipmunks stalking and killing sparrows; a spider-tailed viper that mimics an arachnid to catch birds; muskellunge that eat ducklings; praying mantises eating hummingbirds—*hummingbirds*; and catfish that will attack and eat pigeons right at the shoreline. Wild creatures take what they can—when they can—being the opportunists they are. For instance, it is well known that whitetail bucks and other ungulates shed their antlers in the winter as their testosterone levels fall. This causes a weakening at the pedicle—the base of the antler where it meets the skull—to the point that the horns fall off. One animal's loss becomes another's gain. Squirrels and other creatures take delight in chewing these ornate and accessible skullcaps that once adorned the heads of deer, taking in the divine and elemental nutrients such as calcium and phosphorus, which are vital for maintaining their teeth strength. Since they can't simply *know* that this fine fodder contains a feast of essential minerals, it stands to reason that their instinct is about opportunity, not ferocity.

Once, when I was fishing in the Erie Canal as a boy, I partook of one of the most dumbfounding catches I can ever remember. After casting my lure of choice that day—a yellow and black F-7 flatfish—for some oblivious amount of time through the slow-moving, green-stained waters of June, I began to realize that I could predict its whereabouts before it finally showed itself in the murky water. Perhaps on the fourth or fifth cast, as I envisaged its exact location and speed, I noticed a manifestation appear abruptly and with an alacrity that defied my attempt to both stave it off and comprehend its very presence. Perhaps by now you've guessed it: A medium-sized snapping turtle had come screaming up behind my lure—a lure with three sets of treble hooks—and sucked it into its mouth. Picture yourself in my shoes for a moment: a ten-year-old, alone, fishing off a concrete abutment on the edge of the Erie Canal, now suddenly watching a snapping turtle, who ate his lure full of hooks and kept them inside of its mouth. Luckily for me, the man who lived in the house closest to the water was watching the whole thing and came to my rescue with a kind hand and a pair of needle-nose pliers. Even for a snapper it wasn't that big, but it had some fair-sized claws at the ends of its feet, and now the mouth that normally was fearsome enough on its own had a set of sharp hooks embedded in it.

The kindness of that man has always stayed with me. Thankfully for the turtle, his help meant that it would live to swim another day, despite having a very sore mouth.

———•———

It's an amazing feeling to leave the world for the day and watch nature as it hunts: chickadees and nuthatches chasing food that has become hidden among the November trees, the sound of a woodpecker tearing through the skin of an old oak looking for the summer's leftover and veiled insects, squirrels running the ground beneath me—foraging—while the last leaves fall. Being on this stage alongside them is not about showing or performing, but becoming one with nature's way of hunting; to observe how it's done from the pros of the forests and the waterways, as they dip into rivers to hunt fish or spring into the air and gather insects. Nature hunts in unexpected ways. It's not always an orca chasing a seal right onto the beach, or a pack of wild dogs running down a wildebeest. Hunting animals leap and sometimes land in unexpected places: like a grizzly bear digging for moths high above the timberline, among the bare boulders of Yellowstone; or an owl that hears a snow-burrowed grouse and silently pounces on it from the cover of the pine trees.

In an ever-changing landscape of give and take, the portrait is beautiful and complete before we ever step into the arena. The show is always on.

8

PUTTING OUR TIME IN

It's a phrase we've been telling each other ever since the moment we first went afield, tried our luck, and came back empty-handed. So why does it still bother us every time we hear it?

Perhaps it's because no matter how much time we put in, the results are mixed at best. Despite developing our best observational skills before the season through common reasoning and choosing some grounds over others, the game is not always to be found. It's not that we are ill prepared or have misleading information; it's just that wild animals don't always perform as predicted, which is a good thing. Still, the older I get, the more I feel like I have less time to be wrong about these choices.

Grouse hunting, for instance, consists of walking through different types of cover. Over many years we have learned that sometimes grouse are in an old vineyard, or sometimes sitting in the pines. At other times, they can be spotted coming out from under thorn apple trees. Old, overgrown orchards can garner flushes like walking through an aspen grove.

Often, these different types of cover can be found in the same nearby areas. We may push below the pines all day and have good shooting but never see one in the aspens. Time and effort have told us that in the early fall they tend to be down lower on the hill, walking the old vineyard; while later in the winter they hug the higher elevations, looking for catkins and the cover of the pines.

We began to align these birds' patterns with their various tendencies related to the seasons. But in doing so we found their hiding spots and hunted them with such persistence that we have pushed them even farther away. It's a lesson in overhunting and, as you might have guessed, putting in *too much time*.

As was the case when we were lake shooting duck chasers, watching for weeks while mallards and black ducks (a rarity now, but very huntable in our younger day) were alight in the early morning in a favorite local bay. When opening morning officially came, we had some great wing shooting, but it was the second and third days that told the real tale. By then, the waterfowl had heard the shots ricocheting and were chased from every decent resting spot. We had to find a way to welcome them back, and we knew that it would take some practice. We began to use a few seagull decoys at first (yes, seagulls) as confidence decoys, and when that didn't work out we turned to a great blue heron. And when that too failed, we tried putting a few Canada geese shells on the shore behind us. As time went by we bought tip-ups, a shaker, and finally a battery-powered hen that swam around in the bay! (This was before they came up with flappers, splashers, and full decoy spreader jerk systems.) We learned through trial and error—error being the most apt description—that our calling was too loud and our camouflage incorrect given our surroundings. Though in plain and ostentatious sight, we felt small and helpless.

————·————

That guy Mike I used to hunt with liked to say he was "taking his gun for a walk." I enjoyed the simplicity of that phrase, how it paired innocence and time with the potential aggressiveness of the hunt. It was a phrase wrought with the possibility of failure based upon the many times we had hunted together, and seemingly for little reason other than to do just that: walk with our firearms with little else to do.

When he wasn't around, I started taking my gun for a walk by myself, preferring to concentrate on the walk itself as opposed to the need to shoot at anything. I am, for the most part, a self-taught hunter. My father and my grandfather hunted, of course, but by the time I was ready to seriously learn, their hunting days were receding. For me, this trial-and-error period in my hunting life was fraught with much more error than not. Putting my own time in meant finding what worked by my own means and justifications. Sometimes, it just meant walking.

Walking would lead me to strange places and turn up never-ending surprises.

One of my favorite pastimes was to jump-shoot puddle ducks on ponds where they had been loafing all summer. It was easier than marching during the early hours of the day and setting up decoys, but it wasn't as successful. Setting up and staying there would inevitably garner birds for the game bag, but during the years that I spent in construction, when time was at a premium, the ever-faithful spot-and-stalk method would prove many times to be the key. It's just that most of the time the birds were somewhere else, or had been jumped too many times, making it a lesson in futility that had to be overcome by persistence. Sticking to my plan meant keeping my shotgun in the truck all those years, being that I worked on a mason crew that was always among the first to arrive on the job site of any new home build. Working all those years with a bunch of beer-drinking, monstrously fit, and unkempt "trowel heads" gave me a competitive edge because most of them, if not all of them, also kept their shotguns in their trucks.

If we got off early, the plan was always to find some unknown or unused area to hunt near where we were located, in the attempt to find birds or other game that must surely be hiding there in great numbers. There existed a small but palpable competition among us. The talk during the workday was replete with the hunt to come, or hunts that had already occurred. The stories were there to be shared and bragged about, to be sure, but to not come prepared with one was to be left out.

I was about to make a new one.

One day I was on a job site that was the beginning of a development that would eventually become one hundred houses or more. The roads were in, but the only homes going up were the very few in the front section, along with a model home for the realtors to use as a home base. In the back of the subdivision was a massive pile of topsoil at least fifty yards or more long; this had been stripped from the entire area and saved, with the intention of selling it back to the customers for use in starting their new lawns. On the back side of it was a long, narrow trench made by the earthmovers that had long since stripped the lots of their useful earth; it was a trench that had filled with water.

Looking back from this lonely, muddy, and bedraggled water, one spotted the only wooded area that remained, which thereby divorced the water from, of all things, the expressway. Since it was more than far enough away from the speeding cars (and blocked by the aforementioned woods) to be legal to shoot, and I was always crazy enough to try, I scoped it out just for a grin. There were two mallards, a drake and a hen, sitting in it.

This story isn't so much about me stalking them, jumping them, and then having grilled duck breast that night, as it is about how it would never have happened without the never-ending attempt to find game in an unusual place—and the lesson that carrying my shotgun around in my truck paid off so many times. The individual needs to respond to his or her own propensity to find things out for himself. But, since more eyes see more things, it stands to reason that multiple hunters can learn more and see more as they hunt together. When one of us wasn't paying attention to our surroundings from whatever basement in which we were working at the time, another was. Take, for instance, about ten years later, and barely around the corner from the "duck-expressway" place, when my employer at the time suddenly stood up from the wall on which he was working, pointed his finger, and quietly said, "Check it out."

He had laid his eyes on two of the most glorious rooster pheasants that I had ever seen. Utterly wild birds, the roosters had flown across the road and onto the land that we were working, and they were in the process of brawling like street thugs. The only reason that we didn't immediately set out after them was that my coworker wanted to run home and get his black lab, Shea. My Chase, who accompanied me to work and who was still a rookie at that time, had set upon a few stocked birds, but now she would get her chance at the real deal. The birds would probably get away.

Shea, on the other hand, was a master flusher, and it was my experience that she could find any bird, anywhere.

Once my friend returned, the two birds had disappeared into a ditch, which was all that remained of a former creek. We each took a side and let our girls do their stuff. Amazingly, Chase locked up first, I moved in, and she was on it like glue just a few moments later; it was her first retrieve of a truly wild bird. Shea had the other bird in the air a few minutes later, and both of us had our own pheasant meals that evening.

Allowing Chase the opportunity to put her own time in was something that she had worked for and earned—and in fact needed—to be the dog that she was to become. Eventually, I worked her all the way into the "master hunter" program with a local upland game dog club, but because of time and, sadly, money, she only ever achieved "senior hunter" status, despite my uselessness as a trainer. But a finished gundog she was in my estimation.

Putting your time in is all about faith, and I had faith in Chase. I gladly followed her to the ends of the earth, putting my confidence in her ability to seek the unthinkable, and rarely did she disappoint. Perhaps she had faith in me too.

Faith is, after all, the bedrock of each hunter's success. While it seems that more and more success rejects the *need* for faith, it lingers at the hunter's side like a tried-and-true friend. The hunter may think that continued success has made him self-reliant and interminably confident, but all it has done is given him a temporary badge he wears when things happen to be going well. For all other times, staying faithful to one's practice is necessary when the hours feel like days and the days like years. For the hunter, it is time well served.

Part Three

THE HUNT

One does not hunt in order to kill; on the contrary, one kills in order to have hunted . . . if one were to present the sportsman with the death of the animal as a gift he would refuse it.

—JOSE ORTEGA Y GASSET

THE MOST DIFFICULT GAME

All the jolly chase is here
With hawk and horse and hunting-spear,
Hounds are in their couples yelling,
Hawks are whistling, horns are knelling
—Sir Walter Scott, "Hunting Song"

I've seen at least a hundred beautiful trophy rooms full of the heads of wild game. It's a dizzying sight to behold, a panoramic display for hunters who can't travel the earth in search of game they would love to hunt, and a feather in the cap for those who can. In an unnatural arrangement, elk, moose, and mule deer hang side by side with warthog, leopard, and kudu. It's surprisingly easy to get "lost" in someone else's game room and forget that you are not on the Serengeti or the Kalahari but rather standing inside in the company of another hunter. I've spent hours admiring these immense bounties on display, imagining the hunt that transpired, only to be interrupted by the brazen voice of the hunter: *Wanna know how I got that one?*

Collectively, these trophy hunters' stories melt into colorful tales in which the adventure of taking these difficult-to-hunt creatures is supplanted by boastful, self-congratulatory words. They seek to hide the fact that the skin on the floor or the head on the wall was just as beautiful before it was shot as it is after.

I'm the same as anyone who has seen the bounty on the wall and dreamed of trying his hand at defeating a trophy animal at its own game. I've gutted countless deer in the field by my own hand without anyone showing me how. I've field dressed ducks, geese, grouse, turkeys, rabbits, woodcock, and thousands of fish, but the fact remains that I won't shoot an animal I'm not going to eat.

This is not a rebuke of big game hunters who routinely take animals that aren't very good table fare. Any decent hunter worth his or her good name hunts for a variety of reasons, most of which have been explored in this book. But it does illustrate the paradox found among hunters who say they are conservationists but continue to go trophy hunting. The thrill of the hunt has its own merits, of course, and has been written about many times, in both literature and hunting manuals. But what compels one to pull the trigger, knowing that the animal's fate will be resigned to staring down from a mantel? Is it the long shot, from cliff to cliff; the impossible skill to pull it off from a distance? Is it the dream of going far off the road, on unmarked trails, to find the stunning and unique creatures of which the hunter has only heard stories? Is it a part of defeating nature, a nature that can and will defeat the hunter, sometimes causing his death? It's an uneasy feeling for some hunters to know that other like-minded outdoorsmen will work so hard to find beauty and mystery in a rare animal, even putting themselves in danger for it, only to bring it home as a carcass meant for the wall.

Trophy hunters call it the most difficult game based on the fact that some of the animals they capture live at high altitudes, or in the jungles of Africa, or in remote desert regions or mountainous terrain, and that many pose tangible dangers to humans.

I, however, call this the most difficult game because of the resounding, challenging territory surrounding the practice of trophy hunting and the accept-it-or-be-damned attitude of those within the community itself.

There are many people out there who call themselves big game hunters or hunting guides, who spend years pursuing their chosen trade, while acknowledging the fact that, while their business provides vast funds to conservation, they almost exclusively kill for "sport." The word denotes an activity designed solely to appease the hunter without granting respect to the animals that he loves.

Therein lies the truest definition of the most difficult game: a tenuous, sometimes problematic, and challenging philosophy to justify.

Perhaps no place has better glorified the hunt than the American West. The Lewis and Clark expedition turned hunters into freedom fighters, heralding a time when the hunt was as much about the chase as it was about subsistence. Even those two revered figures in American history had been ordered to keep some part of their hunts as a "trophy" for President Thomas Jefferson. According to the Thomas Jefferson Foundation, Inc., "along with recording in detail their sightings of all types of animals, the exploration party collected skins, horns, entire skeletons." This served as proof of not only a passage to the west but of what they saw and felt and, yes, harvested. They wouldn't have made jewelry or trinkets from the bones, as the Native Americans sometimes did, but when they returned with proof of their expedition it created a passion for those who had never left their farmsteads. It stirred wonder—the same wonder that captivates the hunter to this day.

Of the thirteen different game animals—as we know them today—that the Lewis and Clark mission killed and consumed, at least four of them were species known to grow some type of antler or horn, including deer, elk, antelope, and one that would have surely found a great place in their sights, the bighorn sheep. Today, this big game animal is the stuff of legend in the hunting community. The bighorn sheep may be the single most sought-after trophy in the North American hunting world, based on its difficulty to access and its limited numbers. It's said that Lewis and Clark "saw them on every ridge," but their population has dwindled from nearly 2 million at the turn of the century to around 70,000 today. In 2013, it became more than just a legend when an anonymous hunter bid a record $480,000 for a Montana bighorn sheep tag.

As it is, the bighorn sheep is probably the most difficult and expensive big game tag to procure. In 2014 alone, thanks to data from the Utah Department of Wildlife Resources, some 5,174 Utah hunters applied for 35 desert bighorn tags, while a staggering 7,184 nonresidents vied for a remaining 3. This is proof positive that while the drive to hunt these remarkable wild sheep is alive and well, there remains some concern about their overall numbers. Disagreements around the taking of these rare and spectacular rams range from the strictest conservational claims to those about simple population control, stripped of ethical qualifications. Certainly, enough of those in the scientific community, with an eye toward wildlife biology and management, have stated their willingness to support such a hunt, signified by the fact that the Beehive State still allows it to continue. It stands to reason, then, that when game animals are financially valued, there becomes an incentive to protect them.

If money talks, it speaks volumes about the interest it creates in trophy hunting, particularly sheep. The unique attention created by trade shows, such as the Wild Sheep Foundation's Sheep Show, which display a vast array of trophy mounts, is enough to stir a desire in anyone to pursue any trophy game animals, even though the average hunter may not be able to afford it. A trip, say, to the Yukon or Alaska to hunt a Dall or Stone sheep may range in price from $25,000 to $50,000, while one Michigan man paid an extraordinary $100,000 for a bighorn hunt in Montana. And that amount is a pittance compared to some. Wild sheep tags are auctioned off at the Sheep Show for sums of up to a quarter of a million dollars or more. Played to the gasps and cheers of a live audience. Add to that the giddy elation at the possibility of filling out the tag after a long hunt, and what hunter wouldn't want to be a part of that?

Another realistic perspective in the hunting community has emerged, one that shares the same big hunting objective but with conservation in mind. Not all hunters would care to embark on a trophy ram hunt, preferring to let an animal of such magnificence thrive without his interference. Intense trophy hunting for bighorn sheep is now said to have had an unintended effect on the trait most sought after in the first place: the size of its horns. Unnatural selection by the hunting community may now result in an "artificial evolution," in which the taking of the most mature rams year after year prevents their more developed DNA from spreading to future generations. Other trophy hunters rebuke this, arguing that those same mature rams, having lived for so long, have already spread their seed after many successful mating seasons.

Perhaps the one thing that trophy hunters and non-trophy hunters can agree on is the joining together as outdoorsmen for the ultimate goal: to keep the hunting life—any hunting life— available for future generations that will grow into adulthood across North America and in particular the American West.

For those who might have come of age in the West, hunting was not a mere romantic vision but a way of life. Firsthand experience and encounters with aggressive black bears or grizzlies or rutting bucks in the throes of the breeding season would have made these folks attuned to the need for training on how to properly fire their guns in the chance that something *should* happen. A lifestyle of perpetual threat might have led some to hunt animals beyond the need of simply hunting for meat. As Ernest Hemingway wrote in *Green Hills of Africa*: "I did not mind killing anything, any animal, if I killed it cleanly, they all had to die and my interference with the nightly and the seasonal killing that went on all the time was very minute and I had no guilty feeling at all."

Even when man—man that had already "conquered" nature; post Industrial Revolution man—found out that there were creatures in the world that couldn't and wouldn't be dominated in their own domain, he had to try. When he found out that some of these amazing creatures can and will kill us the first chance they get, he needed to assert his dominance. It didn't take long; in fact, the rift he caused between himself and the nonhunting community still stands. What's needed is a middle ground.

This may sound counterintuitive, but perhaps the best way to preserve and restore such a fierce class of trophy animals may be to allow strictly limited and structured hunting of that species. Take the wild sheep as an example again and the Michigan man who spent $100,000 to hunt the bighorn in Montana: The entire amount went to the Chippewa Cree tribe, on whose reservation the hunt took place and who used it to fund positions for two wildlife conservation officers. In the case of the nearly half-million-dollar tag in the Treasure State, referenced earlier, several hundred thousand of those dollars went directly to the state's fish, wildlife and parks department. Between the wealthy individuals who pay astounding sums for the hunts and the esteemed organizations like the Wild Sheep Foundation that routinely make multimillion-dollar donations—not including several million dollars raised by auction each year—North American big game animal hunters have a more ethical impetus to take healthy populations into the future.

By all accounts, it would seem then that the trophy hunt is truly only a "rich man's game." If so, the average hunter, then, is a dreamer. With the lack of the same capital to create such a hunt for himself, he is limited to a mere surveyor of the big game hunt, his experience condensed to magazine pages and viral videos. Many of these same hunters may procure but one chance in a lifetime to hunt an animal of their dreams, while many still are happy enough to see it on the wall in a museum placed there as an artifact by some erstwhile hunter with a different agenda. These same hunters can still imagine the setup and the shot, see in their mind's eye the recklessly approaching trophy that they are looking at on some wall, now frozen forever by the artistry of the taxidermist. So then for many who can only dream about such a hunt, does the desire, but lack of affordability then cause them to become negative and weary of it? Do hunters who cannot be a part of such a hunt then convert to that which they hate even more: an anti-hunter? It stands to reason that jealousy has some part in all of this, and yet most in the hunting community care even less for the kind of divisiveness that can pit hunting brothers against one another.

While our human instincts demand that we stay away from life-threatening situations, our adventurous spirits tell us otherwise. I'll never purposely hunt a grizzly bear or a mountain lion, but I am a trophy hunter all the same, perhaps for the reason that I continually let small bucks walk by me, over and over, in the blatant attempt to find the most mature buck possible, one with the most points on his antlers. More generally, we cull old trees from the forest in the endeavor to let the younger ones gain more light, even knowing that nature will establish its own hierarchy over time. Trees have a way of reminding the hunter that the old kings of the forest may die and disappear, but it is in their roots and the way that they spread their seeds that they will live forever. The same is true for the animal world.

I know of one Canadian hunter who has successfully taken all the Big Five African game animals: lion, leopard, rhinoceros, elephant, and Cape buffalo. He is currently in the process of having his elephant's legs made into foot stools . . . *foot stools*. He did not want to be named for this book, nor did he want to provide pictures of himself or any of his big game mounts. Perhaps this represents a possible guilt that he is wracked with, compounded by his wish to stay free from fueling the anti-hunting movement. Based on his game room and the exquisite mounts included therein, one can guess he feels proud that he has conquered the unconquerable and is now somehow free from being judged, as long as he stays in the shadows.

Any hunter who keeps his pursuit in the light of the regulations and within the perspective of conservation has nothing to answer to but his or her own conscience, and that's not a difficult game to play at all.

10

OUR BODIES AS HUNTERS

I expect nonhunters to have a difficult time understanding why I live for the hunt, but I'm going to try and help them. I spent many years listening to my family members ask me if I were "going to shoot Bambi" this year. Being a wise guy, I usually replied, "No, not Bambi. Bambi's father." (Sometimes Bambi's mother, if they were really annoying me.) It might have been an insensitive thing to say, but this quip is an old reminder that not all hunters care to feel the ascribed kind of "false humanity" that nonhunters give to the hunt. In other words, they eschew the expectation that they should somehow see everything from the point of view of a fantasist. It's entirely possible that if Pinocchio were a game animal, my family would have asked me if I had cut his strings.

The mythologizing of game is not new or surprising. Throughout history, humans have watched from a distance while the creatures around them killed and maimed and ate each other, so it's not hard to imagine that they began to fine-tune their bodies for the possibility that they might be next. In 1924, the 2.8-million-year-old skull of a young child, dubbed the Taung Child after the area in South Africa in which it was found, was discovered to have holes inside of its eye sockets, similar to the kind found in animals that have been grabbed by an eagle in flight. Among the other discoveries at the site were an odd array of animal bones and egg-shells, encouraging the strength of the hypothesis.

Our ancestors believed that the animal bones early hunters came across gave rise to the possibility that all sorts of fearsome creatures were out there, not the least of which could still be lurking in their natural surroundings, waiting to strike them down. Stanford University historian Adrienne Mayor, for example, has been instrumental in documenting the relationship between Native Americans and the fossil bones they discovered, and she explains how the myth of the Thunder Bird may have arisen due in part to the discovery of Tyrannosaurus rex bones and the (mis)understanding on the part of those peoples that the skeletal remains must be something out of this world. To this day, human beings still find strange things washed up on the shores of the earth's oceans and argue over their origins. The limits of our imaginations are as expansive as the animal kingdom is strange.

Eventually, however, fear evolved into pragmatism, and some of the early weapons that hunters made were created from sharp skeletal pieces, which made them capable of defending themselves. Humans learned to assuage their fears and fortify their determination, banding together to hunt by the same methods long used by the predacious creatures they had observed in the first place; they learned to use their bodies proactively instead of reactively. This approach enabled them to be both more successful and athletic, and they donned the visage of competitor rather than spectator.

Modern-day hunters can commence their pursuit with much less fear of being ejected into the category of nothingness. Kaput. Still, the brutal physicality of the work often reminds them of their distant origins, even if it does no more to remind them of their safety.

———— • ————

Back in the early part of the 1980s I traveled to the North Country—a landlocked area near the St. Lawrence River—to duck hunt a beaver swamp with an old friend, John. His family owned an island out on the river, but this spot was inland, somewhere between the river and the famed Black Lake. To get out to the island we loaded our weary young selves and our two shotguns into a fourteen-foot rowboat that was mounted with a fifteen-horsepower outboard motor, and we rode the short distance out into one of the most famous rivers in North America.

Before we left home, my friend had made his mind up that, for at least one of the days that we were there, we were going to set up in a swamp that was well off the road. It was an area in which he and his older brother were known to chase grouse, which they were in the middle of pursuing one day when they chanced upon a small beaver pond that was full of mallards laying over from the migratory journey south.

Once out there, the issue was not of mental fortitude but of getting our bodies to comply. It was time to work. While my hunting friend was stronger and could carry a load greater than I could, he wasn't going to offer to take more. I soon discovered how far my arms and legs could carry bags of decoys and a shotgun through the woods and over rocky shale-laden mounds, all the while wearing an old pair of chest waders. Bending at the waist to get through the trees while keeping a power grip on a gun with no sling and decoys while following someone in the dark—to a place that you've never been before—is like closing your eyes and imagining yourself trying to swim through a school of fish without arms.

From under my sweat-laden gaze, I watched my legs stumble in anguish, then felt my arms burn as we carried on under the pine boughs and by the sumac. It wasn't until we eyed the swamp that we let gravity offload our belongings.

Before we could sing praises to the Lord above for taking these weighty burdens from us, the task at hand became the strategic placement of decoys ahead of the oncoming sunrise. Our hands took over for our feet and began to pull the varied cork-and-plastic imitation mallards out of the bags and separate them from twine and anchor. My friend worked diligently with a flashlight that he lodged inside his mouth, and I began to move my aching legs in and out of the water with a decoy in each hand. One of his classic cork decoys distinctly hit the water right next to me in the dark, causing me to question my partner's motive in tossing one. He simply said, "I didn't throw anything." I learned then that in the black of a predawn morning, in a North Country swamp, a beaver—angry with an intruder—will slap its flat, waffle-patterned tail on the water to let you know that you're an unwelcome trespasser.

We're not that young anymore, and we have both found out many times over the years how much abuse our bodies can take when it comes to the hunt, but that knowledge didn't accumulate without a lot of experience. Between treading the hills of New York's Southern Tier in search of grouse and deer, and hunting the swamps and shoals of the mighty St. Lawrence River for waterfowl, we tried to mitigate our movements to ease the passing of our hunt.

One of the first places I learned to set up a mass of decoys—

known to duck hunting veterans as a "block"—was on the shores of Lake Ontario in a state park called Lakeside Beach. I had come to that spot—at different times—with the aforementioned friend, his brother, and at least five or six other people, since it was one of the few state parks that I knew of in New York that allowed hunting at that time, though there were strict rules involved. The most difficult of these was the law requiring us to park our vehicles in the lot provided by the park service, which was at least half a mile or more from the point that we preferred to hunt. In the beginning, we simply trudged the entire distance with a few bags of decoys, dropped them off, and came back for more. There was no bending at the waist or straining to get through the trees or rocky outcroppings. Other than some tall grass out in the field, it was wide open, albeit insanely lengthy. At times we could skirt a gate that was at one end, meant only for the parks department trucks, which allowed them access to those far reaches of the wilder parts of the park via a dirt road. This gave us a reprieve to drop everything off, then we drew straws to see who had to take the truck or car back to the lot and march back on foot.

In those early years, we hunted that area mostly during the "second season" after Christmas. I have already expressed some small part of my heart and soul in this book based on the hunts that we undertook there: the incredible sight of hundreds of different kinds and masses of waterfowl and the feelings this engendered in me. As you can imagine, the success we had there was beyond a young hunter's ability to grasp, and it was the biggest reason I began to spend my early masonry-made money on gear to make it even better. At one point I bought four-dozen bluebill decoys to add to all the "dekes" my other friends had. We used a few bags, yes, but since we had so little money at our disposal, we also used laundry baskets, an old metal tub, and several plastic garbage cans that I had either procured from my parents or bought myself. I didn't have the extra money to spend on the proper cord or something as specialized as grapple anchors, so I improvised with what I had on hand: cotton laundry-line rope and an odd collection of barbell weights.

Imagine stuffing fifty or so decoys into this misshapen array of bins, lifting them up with five- and ten-pound barbell weights lying at the bottom, and carrying them half a mile in the dark at around four o'clock in the morning. Maybe the best part was stepping off the cliff where the grass ended, perched above the lakeshore like an evil sand castle—possibly twenty feet tall—and trying to scramble downhill to the water without falling. If you've ever tried to hold down lines of decoys, tethered together in groups of five or six at a time, in the pounding surf of a stiff northwest wind, you'll understand the use of such an odd method to anchor your decoys, especially for young men with very little money to spend and the draw of a hunt of which they can't get enough. It's the same reason hunters tread outside in the frost of January to the shore of the Great Lakes, their extremities freezing and body shivering, until their functions diminish in efficiency.

Being in good physical condition—maybe one of the few things over which the hunter has the most control—reduces his urge to quit, just as strict mental resilience curtails the numbness in his feet or the aches in his back. The hunter can easily become caught up in what he *hopes* will happen before it ever does happen, causing his eyes to focus on the wrong area at the wrong time. Mental strength is the difference between responding to these distractions and eventually reaching his goal. In the interim, the body responds to torrents of pressure, stumbling in the dark and the wind and the rain.

Opposable thumbs may be a part of our very evolution, but I swear they were expressly made for the hunter. As an outdoorsman, he has displayed them in the up position to express victory, but they are best suited for pulling up his boots and tying his laces with authority. They work exceedingly well to cover the hands with gloves and apply shooting glasses to the face. They raise the duck call to his lips or together make the wand and slate sing out in turkey breeding ecstasy. Their use for gripping and dragging a carcass is only matched by their numb clutch of his frozen decoys, shotgun shells, and possibly his radio. They are there to be blown on, jammed into a tree, or cut by his favorite knife, small infractions for the glory of the pursuit. They are best suited to grip his friend's hand in exultation or his firearm in familiarity. (I do not mean to leave out the many disabled hunters who enjoy the hunt to the fullest thanks in part to modern accessories. Those without the use of their legs can still make it into the great outdoors with all-terrain means of transportation, for example.)

It goes without saying that the body requires a certain stamina in order to hunt. The eyes grow tired after watching the woods and fields for so long, as do the legs after a long walk. The same can be said for the arms that work overtime upon seeing his quarry walk into firing range, how they stall as he observes his firearm clutched against gravity or his bow at a tense full draw. And yet the hunter is determined: He will only have to remind himself that should his body hesitate, his mind must persist. After all, it's been a gracious partner throughout all the blows he has received in life.

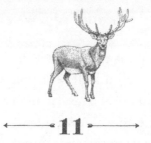

ARROGANCE OF THE POACHER

We've talked at length about hunters' egos, and how the stories they tell themselves and each other are often more glorious than their actual pursuits. Similarly, the poacher lives in this fantastic world, desiring to cheat the system at any cost, thereby defining himself in a way contrary and abysmal to the rest of us. He takes the shot after the legal shooting season is over—the hen when only drakes are allotted or a buck after he has already procured one. In a world characterized by self-regulation and the observance of common hunting virtues, when he is alone and unfettered by the law, he consistently disregards it. He is undeserving of the moniker "hunter" and all the respect that comes with it.

The poacher is mentally and spiritually bereft. He tethers himself to the lie that his victory over nature takes precedence over the actual hunt. He disregards game laws that he feels don't fit with his bullish ideology; he is addicted to success and finds any tangible way to fulfill his fascination with it. Ironically, he has mostly been a failure as a hunter and has found that the way to evade this is by creating his own rules.

The average hunter, meanwhile, has shown that he can walk away from either success or failure with poise. The laughter he hears upon telling how he fell short is about camaraderie rather than humiliation. Conversely, the poacher mainly hears *quietude*. Arrogance deafens his ears to censure. The poacher's impudence in reaping more than his fair share is relative to establishing his self-image, even if it means disavowing his conscience. In his desire to display beautiful head mounts in his game room, while knowing his tactics are illegal, he hides behind a veil of ignorance, believing himself invisible.

He's not, though. He's utterly passionate, despite his lack of respect for the quarry. Here is where the difference between poacher and hunter becomes unclear. While the poacher does not care for the accountability of wildlife management or conservation, he possesses the correct licenses and pays his fair share of fees. He has even been an ethical hunter in the past but has tripped over good fortune and let it get the best of him: His taking of too many ducks after a morning hunt was replicated time and time again.

I can remember as far back as the mid-1970s listening to our neighbor's son brag about slaughtering the smallmouths on open-ing morning of the season and keeping thirty or forty when the daily limit was five fish. His lack of respect for the law was as-tounding. He would only come in off the water for a rest before going back out and destroying them again. And since poaching knows no borders, there was a wealthy Canadian I met who told me the story of how he had procured vast acreage on the border of Ontario's revered Algonquin Park when he was a younger man. The hundreds of acres came with its own lake, full of speckled trout, and land that held moose, black bear, and deer. He relayed to me how it was becoming more difficult to see bear because he and the men who hunted his land with him had shot so many (while whispering to let me know that it was okay because he had already taken three that spring). Not lost on me was the fact that in the basement of his home was a butchering room with every possible feature, kept busy by the deer he shot as they came out of the woods to eat the apples from the trees in his yard.

Poaching is not limited to the taking of animals. In the for-ests of Wisconsin, for instance, citizens have begun cutting down birch trees on public lands thanks in part to several well-known craft-driven websites and, ironically, the yearning to bring some of the natural world inside. The wish to adorn their homes with the branches and limbs of lovely white-barked "paper" trees means trading decoration for decorum. In California, poachers have been targeting redwoods for their old-growth burls, whose intricate patterns are highly prized. Venus flytraps, which have an extremely limited natural home range in the Wilmington, North Carolina, area, are disappearing due to poachers who only want to sell them as pets. Even ginseng growing wild in the Smoky Mountain National Park on the border of North Carolina and Tennessee can fetch as much as $800 a pound on the black market, leading to a plethora of illegal activity.

Conversely, the Ojibwe, part of the Chippewa nation, legally spear walleye during the fish's spring spawning run in Wisconsin—a traditional right in their culture. The Northern Arapaho tribe in Wyoming kill bald eagles for religious purposes to use in their annual Sun Dance ceremony, even though it is the U.S. national symbol.

So, is poaching just the destructive side effect of illegal hunting, or the semantics of two sides disagreeing?

In North America, poaching methods speak volumes about the mind-sets of the individuals performing these acts. In 2014, four men were charged with illegally taking an elk on private property that was not open to hunting; two of the men were, at that time, employed by the U.S. Fish and Wildlife Service. The courts ruled that the pair were complicit in poaching the animal on the Roan Plateau in Colorado.

Cases like this one are often local stories and are seldom reported on a national level. In large states comprised of vastly remote areas like Colorado, Wyoming, Montana, and Utah, to name just a few, poaching stories are big news, whereas in urban metropolises they fall by the wayside. Our culture's consumerist mentality dictates that these stories are not big moneymakers, so they are shunned in favor of bigger, attention-grabbing headlines. Meanwhile, the regular destruction of nature continues.

There may be nothing that draws the ire of the hunter more than a braggart spewing his shallowness over ill-gotten game, who responds in kind by letting everyone else know who is doing the talking and why. It's a straightforward way in which those of us in the hunting community get the message out. Word of mouth is a sharp knife that can cut the poacher and bring his misdeeds into the open.

Authorities on the front lines of the fight have been listening and are now beginning to use high-tech methods to fight these crimes. For instance, full-sized robotic deer and other faux mechanical animals are now being placed in many states to derail poaching at its core in remote areas. These life-sized and motorized mechanical wonders are positioned along roadsides in rural areas, where undercover environmental law enforcement officers sit in wait for poachers to shoot at them either out of season or many times after dark. They are often taxidermied animals that have real exteriors, such as fur or feathers, along with an inner mechanism that is controlled by remote. Two companies in Wisconsin come to mind: Robotic Decoys and Custom Robotic Wildlife have been selling animatronic creatures to wildlife authorities across North America, and it's starting to pay off. Footage abounds of wildlife officers swooping down on illegal roadside shooters and poachers of all types. Six different people were caught in Skagit County, Washington, alone during the 2017 deer season by WDFW authorities using a robotic deer decoy. Arizona, Utah, Indiana, and Missouri are just a few of the states now busting wildlife poachers with these decoys by placing them in remote locations and setting up surveillance over them. In New York, the state Department of Environmental Conservation has used pheasant decoys to nab offenders.

Hunting organizations across the land respond similarly. Their websites post articles about heinous acts of poaching, displaying names, locations, fines, and even jail time incurred. They host live functions that educate, and they are allied with wildlife law enforcement, in some cases even offering chat boards on websites that give some anonymity to those meek few who would like to report but still treasure their privacy.

———

The history of the poacher is infused with tales of illegal hunts and game taken to the extreme, but it may have started as the underprivileged peoples of the world purely trying to survive.

European peasants illegally hunted the lands of the wealthy to find food for their families and were eventually allowed to hunt smaller game on their own farms. The Robin Hood of folklore was said to have rescued the serfs who were caught poaching King John's wild beasts.

Poaching has since evolved into a problem no longer connected to poverty but to opportunity and even thrill seeking. In early 2017, ten people were arrested in a sting in the northwestern United States. After over a hundred animals had been killed, with many left to rot, wildlife authorities were rewarded when two of the offending individuals were captured in the act by the remote cameras that had been set up. Some twenty search warrants later, ten poachers were charged in what has now been called "some of the worst [crimes] Washington Fish and Wildlife have ever seen."

What is it that makes a normally decent person addicted to the easy kill? Unfortunately, for the rest of us, the poacher's trespasses aren't noticeable until the damage is done, though our goal is to heed the call long before the woods go bare. There may be no easy answers, but if, as the writer Jan Werich once said, "Arrogance is a hairpiece for covering up an intellectual bald spot," then the poacher must surely have a cold head.

THE HEART AND SOUL
OF REFLECTION

The Buddhists call it *Ānāpānasati*, or "mindfulness of breathing," but the hunter calls it *the woods*. Alone in them he experiences total focus, an effect that limits his breathing to mere nonbreathing, as natural as the wind. Yet even the impatient peoples of the world can peacefully submit to the outdoors when they're alone in the woods. Solitude and mindfulness are states best thought of as paths that only the monk or holy man walks, but when the hunter dives into the outdoor world he changes from carpenter to vicar, from mason to friar, and becomes as invisible as the bark on every tree.

Even when he's not a part of the pursuit, the hunter sees moments that give him pause to reflect: one hundred geese diving like a waterfall into a thawed mid-March pond occupied by one thousand of their brothers and sisters, wings pumping in a retro-rocket motion trying to avoid each other; or the sight of a buck standing openly near the cover of the woods, inexplicably still adorned by his antlers so late after the season. The mere observation of these occurrences—sans action—makes him feel refreshed. If you're aware of the quirky trend called forest bathing, you're also aware that it's nothing new to hunters: We have been wandering since we were old enough to know what it meant to get lost, surrendering to our desire to go missing in plain sight. In the early 1980s, forest bathing became a part of the Japanese public consciousness. Since picnicking under the cherry blossoms was already a national pastime for the Japanese, it is easily understood how the country's forest ministry coined the phrase to garner an even greater desire to get outdoors. Ritual and instinct converged into recreation.

It began with a walk through the quiet of a new-fallen snow. The soft crunch of the flakes released the mind from the unease of everyday life. The incoming amber light signaled the start of day. Lost eventually became known as being found. As he grew into modern man, the hunter became more thoughtful and vigilant about his surroundings. He began to reflect on the outdoors more than any other aspect of his life. It was here that he started to see the world for what it was and what he needed to be thankful for. This he called *reflection*.

Reflection is the ability to look outside oneself to learn something new, but learning never begins until the psychological barriers come down. Then the hunter can accept something that he never before believed as fact, and either change it in himself or let the change happen naturally. This can be as simple as the way he learned to hold his firearm, or as eye-opening as a new attitude toward the way that he regards his immune system. Take for instance *phytoncides*, a word coined in 1928 by Russian biochemist Dr. Boris P. Tokin to describe a substance trees emit in order to protect themselves from, among other things, various insects. Their effect on the human body is to increase NK (natural killer) cell activity in the immune system, effectively lasting for a month after a walk in the woods. Perhaps this is exactly why kids get such a high from making tree forts, or why deer hunters love hunting out of them.

If nature is meant to heal and soothe and restore the hunter, then it must be his duty to prescribe the same in return. Connection to nature makes us more self-aware and grants us the capacity to identify with the creatures that we hunt, and we eventually create a more complete unity with other hunters. One or two walks at a time are not enough to convey the hunter's sense of belonging;

he must travel the woods and fields in such a way that he proves to nature that he truly does belong as a member and not as an outsider.

For me, it all began with a single tree. I've hunted the same one now for the last ten years, in an old-school tree climber called the Tree Lounge. It is a mere nineteen pounds of aluminum frame and seatbelt-type straps that can be carried in or out of the woods at will, depending on how I wish to use it. The seat, where the hunter really lies down, is made from nothing more than a black piece of tightly woven fabric that is remarkably strong and supple, even in the cold weather. It requires a fairly straight trunk, reasonably narrow, with no limbs for at least twenty feet to have a chance to disappear from the eyes of deer, but in the sparsity of the November woods nothing can hide forever.

I come to this tree constantly over the course of the year, rain or shine, summer or winter. It is a white ash that is straight and tall, a lean survivor of many decades that happened to start its seed on the high side of the swampy water that always lingers there. Its only wounds, easily seen whenever I visit, are from the battle scars I have carved in its bark over the years due to my inchworm style of climbing with a brazen array of metal and cinch straps.

I consider this tree a friend. I have trimmed her branches and shaved her bark, yet she still accepts me. I have pruned the neighbors around her and given her light, cutting nothing to the ground more than limb and leaf. This has caused the animals to come nearer in an acceptance of the new paths now easily seen and gladly traversed. There is now community where there was once only undergrowth and resistance; the tracks of new animals that glide by are now customary not erroneous; and as I sit twenty feet above, day after day, in solitude and reflection, I realize that these creatures are now coming to me instead of the other way around.

Is it simply a matter of putting my time in, the vast period spent in the same wild place over the course of the season? Or has this location accepted my ritual without just tolerating my intrusions? The origins of topiary date back to Roman times, and yet I cannot help but feel that my simple pruning has made this place a little better—me along with it. I don't see deer every time I come to this place, but I see many more now than I did in the beginning. Coming here after a snowfall displays even more of what is there when I am not: highways of tracks that cannot be seen in the leaf litter, the movement of animals after dark, tree and ground rubs that were never there in years past.

There are many hunters out there who do not feel so refined by the world from which they take. There are cigarettes smoked, wrappers flung, and shell casings left to rust in the newly fallen snow. These who have had their fair share of success are always a mystery to the mindful hunter, begging the question: How is it that nature can give itself to those who seem to regard it only as a resource and not a blessing? For some the taking of an animal's life is not as important as the reason why, achievement being the dominant motive. It stands to reason that they have never had the same care and nurturing blood in their veins that allows them to see and feel their surroundings, causing them to be separated from them. They are a product of a simple desire to hunt, one that replaces mindfulness with self-appreciation, eventually letting it get the best of them. Success happens to them in spite of themselves, but it does not last. It leaves them searching for a connection they cannot find, hence the poacher.

Nature does not understand the difference. Eventually, this separated hunter responds to how sound, smell, and sight make animals react, and he will ultimately be able to counter those senses and encounter game by default. The difference for the hunter who has come to terms with his surroundings is to have this awareness despite the animal's senses.

The outdoor world is complex and vivacious. The hunter does not try to tame nature by taking its energy. Instead he has a primal need to organize it and put it in its place so that it is not a threat. By letting go at times of the impulse to kill, he attempts to merge with his environment in the hope of immersing himself in it but not controlling it. He seeks equilibrium between a passion for the animals in the world and his intense love of the hunt. Not many hunters will sit on a zafu cushion for hours meditating, but even the most masculine hunter can experience kindness toward the natural world.

Hunting is meditation that transcends our ability to define it. It may be said that, since our world is round, it has no beginning and no end, but not so with the hunter or the animals that he hunts. Eventually all things come to their natural end: the hunt, the animals, and the hunter himself. By then, he will bask in a hypnotic glow, like the feeling of being close to a burning fire. In the waning moments of the fire his visage is adorned with a smile, as if all the complexities of the universe can be finally laid to rest.

The hunter who always comes home with meat is a thief.

—BANTU PROVERB

Part Four

THE HARVEST

FOR LOVE OF THE
GAME HARVEST

The game is about to begin.

The off-season provided much in the way of activities that kept our minds and fingers happy—lining up an imaginary shot on any passing bird or watching the ducks in the swampy end of the lake—but now that the hunt is an impending reality, the butterflies are back.

I mean those nerves, those unconquerable flutters that reach into the muscle tissue of the stomach. It's a fleeting thing to be ruined by our nerves one second and feel dominion over them in the next. Yet this is the hunter's experience after having shelved the hunt over the summer, reliving it only vicariously through memory, word of mouth, and the occasional printed page.

The hunt is a delirious throwback to ancestry and its unique customs, best symbolized by the place that he and his family gather almost daily: the dinner table. Seated at the head of this "spiritual throne," he educates those around him about how he came by his meat and, most important, why. He recites testimonies to those he regards in the highest, regaling them with stories of his sheer command of the hunt and all that comes with it.

The harvest is personal and comes with a range of emotions, sometimes diametrically opposed to each other—one moment sharing reverence for an animal, the next in utter anticipation of taking its life. The meal before him cannot utter its own version of the story, so the hunter feels responsible for discussing the hunt's implications—how life begets death, and vice versa—and the problems and solutions it entails. The proverbial table of plenty has made the hunter hungry for additional stories, since the conclusion of one begets the start of another.

A new season arrives at the tail end of last year's exhaustion. We've long since eaten all our game reserves from the previous season, even though we have new recipes on our minds. Our dogs are tired of the waiting too. Every time we open the door to go outside, they think we are about to go afield, and we must meet their forlorn eyes every time with a less than satisfactory look of our own. (Whenever I released Chase out the door, her first reaction was to take ten steps, stop, look, and listen. She hunted our lawn like a pro, sure that her next directive would come in the form of my command or at least something that caught her nose like a grappling hook. I always shared any wild bird meat with her in which she was a part of the pursuit. I would relish her longing eyes as I cut venison into strips to make jerky, always tossing her a few to remind her that she was family and not just some mindless animal good only for my pack-leader's voice. Many times it was just the two of us, mounting my four-wheeled steed to ramble our way to hidden pastures and forests in the effort to make a new memory and fill another much-needed bag.)

Everything is alive now. We gather in groups to make sure that each of us has what it takes, that we are prepared to do what must be done. Our customary prehunt phone calls, texts, and emails can only go so far, and they can never take the place of our exulted hunt: that expressly needed desire to be deeply entrenched by the thought of the woods, however alone we may be once we get afield.

And when we return, we do so glad-handed, our souls fat and happy from success, our elation tempered by the knowledge that we have done our very best to respect our game with a clean kill. The taste for the hunt of our wild game is in direct proportion to the desire to pursue it; in fact, the taste of our wild game increases exponentially by the effort put forth in directing it onto our plates. As hunters, we share in the knowledge and belief that respect for and use of game meat is responsible and has a usable benefit. It most certainly tastes better the harder it is to come by.

Early North American man celebrated the animals that he hunted. He could be spiritual beyond his place in time and history, even praying in some fashion before he ever set out. Hunting was a part of a community affair of planning, sharing skills, and then stalking, killing, and distributing the bounty for all. Without the rest of the community's participation, the hunt could never have occurred as successfully. Techniques such as stalking and driving game or setting up in silence for an ambush were easily discussed and agreed to by everyone; success was an event that could be planned for as well as discovered.

In more modern times, the nomadic Beothuk people of Newfoundland, said to have disappeared by 1829, have a mysterious yet beguiling history. These tall, handsome natives with black hair and dark eyes were especially adept when it came to the gathering and preservation of food. They hunted caribou, deer, seal, and even speared salmon and lobster. They built smokehouses to dry and store the flesh of the ground-dwelling animals along with the fish. Any extra meat was wrapped in birch-rind boxes and packages and stored frozen for winter. These amazing people also boiled bird eggs and made a kind of sausage that was stuffed into animal intestines, a precursor to how it is done today. Their efforts, even when handled by individuals, were communally minded.

My son was seven or eight years old the first time I gave him wild meat. I had carefully prepped some venison a couple of nights before, cutting steak into strips and then letting it swim in a vat of my homemade marinade overnight. After twelve hours in a dehydrator—a bit long for some, perfect for me—I peeled each succulent piece from the individual trays, one at a time, and began to pack it into baggies of various sizes. It has always been my belief that the best way to honor something is to preserve it—to, in a way, make it last forever.

I remember my son digging his teeth into the dried meat and tearing it off with his canines and incisors, chewing it for several moments before his face lit up in delight. Now at the age of twenty-four, and a college degree behind him, he'll text me on a whim, a hello or greeting unnecessary: "Got any of that jerky that you make?"

Before he ever sat down to the table, my son felt it an honor and a necessity to take the plate of his father's success into his hands and, thereby, into his life. He desired the ability to share in what he viewed as the embodiment of his father's hard work in the hunt: not because he felt that he had to, but because he wanted to.

The dinners at my home were frequent when my son was young, and less so as he got older. When it came to family dinners at my mother's house, I can still picture my brother's three kids—

the two older boys and my niece—happily asking me questions about my hunts and all they entailed. The boys were usually curious as to my exploits in the woods and fields, longing for answers to mysteries with twinkles in their eyes. One of my greatest loves was portioning the vast tidings of my hunts with them, then always making sure to follow with tales of succulent steaks, bags of freshly made jerky, and tenderloins—oh, the tenderloins—that melt in your mouth and leave you longing for more.

Where my nephews were born explorers, my niece was the one who asked me the obligatory Bambi question every single year. Still, she was inquisitive about my feeling toward the hunt even when she could not get past the idea of consuming a piece of wild meat, although the grocery store stuff was still on the menu. Intensely smart and acutely empathetic, her distaste for the hunt as a food source was offset by her wanting to hear stories around the table. If there's ever a way to involve nonhunters in the hunt, it's at the table over a good glass of wine and conversation.

The table is a celebration. Perhaps the nonhunters of the world—my niece and other friends included—find this the most reasonable way to connect to it via this form of sharing. My wish is to express the intimate relationship that I have to the world around the animals that I hunt, but stories I share of the kill work only to desensitize their feelings about it, not change their minds. I've learned, over time, that this is okay. Enveloped in the laughter of conversation and in between the bites of freshly made sausage lies the question I have always answered affirmatively and they negatively: *Could I do it?* In this way, hunting doesn't need to answer all the questions, but it seeks to examine the connectedness among all living things.

———•———

I still remember my mother's glee when I brought home the first wild turkey that I ever shot, carrying it by the legs, my fingers clutching at its spurs for grip and feeling them dig into my hands. She was ecstatic at the thought of butchering this wild bird, this throwback to her days growing up on the ranch in Nebraska that had been the symbol of strength for her as a young woman. I could now be only a party to the dressing of the bird.

This was a joy for her, not a task. Knife in hand and a broad smile on her face, she dug in with the experienced hands of an older woman, with a confidence and nimbleness that seemed directed not only by her memory, but by someone half her age. The feathers flew around in a disorganized manner that contrasted with the deft strokes of her form. She even separated meat from the tendons and ligaments in an effort to procure every last bit of flesh from the bone and sinew, knowing that to waste any of this hard-earned bird was to thumb our noses at providence and invite the possibility of never enjoying one again.

It took its place in the oven and was roasted to a delicious perfection, welcoming all who would dare to try its delectable portions. And when we savored the bites, we looked toward my mom with wordless love and appreciation. She knew we didn't have to say anything, but the broad smile on her face spoke volumes.

LOVING ANIMALS VS. FEARING ANIMALS

There's no doubt that the hunter has an immense love for the wild creatures of the world, particularly the ones he chases. But those who pursue for the pure rush of the kill, and who do not share in this love, are undeserving of the badge. They are but a small and crass community of faux ideologists whose determination is that all animals were created solely for their gain.

Conversely, there are hunters who make it their business to seek out and study the very same animals they hunt with a determination to create in them a healthy and sustainable population. Their desire to be custodians of that which they choose to pursue makes for feel-good stories, but sometimes these best intentions re-create the same problems they are trying to resolve.

Take, for instance, in 2008 when wildlife authorities in Alligator Point, Florida, were called in to take responsibility for a rogue black bear that had wandered into a residential neighborhood. When the biologists sunk a tranquilizer dart into the back hip of the large and mobile bruin, their good intentions to return the big bear to the Osceola National Forest were thwarted when it dashed to the nearby water and began to swim away as the sedative was taking effect.

Enter one intrepid wildlife biologist by the name of Adam Warwick and his will to prevent this Florida black bear from drowning. After watching it flounder, he jumped in and grabbed the four-hundred-pound bear while keeping its head up and swimming some twenty-five yards to shore. With the help of a work crew, a backhoe was used to pluck the bear off the ground and into a pickup truck for the trip back to the bruin's home. The bear was saved, demonstrating that there are outdoorsmen who have an unlimited love for the animals in their keep.

Outdoorsmen have a knack for finding these situations due to their familiarity with their surroundings; they know what to look for, even when not looking for it, and know how to react, even when fate would provide an unpleasant scenario. Let's discuss how whitetail fawns will emerge around June, and how the hunter is as sad as anyone upon seeing one dead on the side of the road or, worse, in the jaws of a coyote. Hunters do not have exclusive rights to know that animals like whitetail deer are caught in the throes of this precarious balancing act of our natural world, but their unique perspective—that of the fair chase—demands that they understand the drive it takes to find these animals while keeping themselves safe. We educate ourselves to the best of our abilities and usually consider three options: whether to hunt animals, study them, or, in some cases, avoid them.

Hunters in western mountainous regions who possess a lifetime of knowledge imparted by their hunting elders understand that this also brings them into dangerous circumstances that chill them to the bone: This is bear territory, after all. A dense forest or alpine meadow near the greater Yellowstone ecosystem may be the stalking areas of the *Ursus arctos horribilis*, but it is also home to some of the best elk hunting that can be had. Hunters there have grown up appreciating the supreme grace of mist that covers their mountainside blind with a rolling fog. The aspens quaking among the downed trees and logs exude cool air that is shrouded in the mystery of a bugling, thousand-pound animal with a head full of antlers that could spear you dead in an instant and yet disappear without a trace right in front of you. And yet the man with the bow or the rifle is not the only hunter here.

There are stories concerning hunters who wanted to harvest what they could for the use of their family, only to be ambushed by one of nature's mightiest creatures, the grizzly bear. In late

October 2017, a woman and her hunting guide were field dressing an elk on public hunting land near Cody, Wyoming, when a large grizzly interrupted the process and attacked them both, sending them to the hospital with non-life-threatening injuries. The bear, it seems, took one of the quartered elk pieces and left. Its hunt now over, it withdrew in peace.

A month later, a Montana man had the same "luck" in an area north of Yellowstone National Park known as Paradise Valley. As he was quietly tracking through the new-fallen snow an elk that he had shot the night before, a grizzly appeared from behind some nearby bushes and immediately came at him. As the bear was trying to protect an elk that now belonged to him, the hunter was relatively lucky to have received only a bite to his right arm and some scratches on his face. In both cases, wildlife authorities and the injured people in question agreed that no further action should be taken against the bears, as they understood this: The bears were protecting a natural food supply, and it was the hunters, in fact, who were in bear country.

Knowing that a great and uncommon animal such as the grizzly is an integral part of the niche in which it lives, hunters have a great desire to protect it and its kind, including the wilderness in which it spends its life. But what about creatures that exist easily within our reach? When a rutting whitetail buck is in an extreme phase of the breeding season, and his body is in the throes of ungulate passion, he can be both easy to fool and as dangerous as it gets. When the deer hunter plots his way toward the taking of one of these normally wily and steadfast deer, he cannot take for granted the possibility that it won't attack at the scent of a rival—a scent that many in the deer hunting community use directly on their person. Even for me, the sight of a fawn in the spring is heartwarming. Watching one struggle to follow its mother in its early days allows me to forget about how much I love deer hunting and let the chase go for a while, giving me time to consider: Will this fawn become a buck or doe? In a buck's very first autumn, with its initial antlers beginning to show—only as faint nubs—my eyes don't see a target but a baby. Should it grow into a doe, there is every chance that someday it will become a mother to twins and start the whole process anew some June not far around the corner. This all belies the underlying fact that as a veteran hunter, I still see deer in my dreams and hope to lay my vision upon a mature deer that has grown a head of horns that would look great on the wall. My love for the whitetail is one that gives rise to a meditation in patience and quiet reflection, all beginning with the simple sight of a fawn in spring.

We can both love and fear these amazing creatures: have them in our world as a living and sustainable animal for generations to come, and hunt them within the bounds of reasonable safety.

You would be hard pressed to find anyone who hasn't heard of the spectacular bison and its incredible comeback story. Even though there is a difference between buffalo and bison—bison being native to North and South America, buffalo to Africa and Asia—nearly everyone concurs that these spectacular herding animals, who were on the brink of extinction at the turn of the century, are now more than just the folklore of the American West. Conservation efforts to restore the populations of the mighty "buffalo" have reaped a much-acknowledged success, as well as an interesting but dangerous side effect: Since around 1980 more than three times as many people in Yellowstone National Park alone were injured by bison than by bears, often due to a desire to take pictures of them, particularly selfies. Now the bison has done so well that hunts for this massive animal are becoming routine in many western states.

Another Yellowstone animal, the wolf, has an undeserving ill reputation, but the animal has become synonymous with ecological resurrection and, as some call it, *trophic cascade*. This refers to the interaction that occurs when predators in an ecosystem hunt and thereby curb the population of their prey (in this case, elk and deer); this alters the behavior of the prey, moves them out of certain areas, and prevents the next lower "trophic level"—here, the plants—from being decimated. In 1995, the seldom loved and oft-hunted wolf was reintroduced into the most famous park in the contiguous United States, starting a chain reaction that is still one of the most remarkable on record. When the wolves again began killing deer and elk, they were giving life to a host of plants. The chain reaction (part of a scientific philosophy once described as "how wolves change rivers") explains that when the valleys and river edges were made free of elk and other ungulates—and their constant and unrelenting feeding—a rebirth of vegetation occurred that changed the landscape. The regeneration that ensued over the course of a few years caused trees to more than triple in height, the ground to host plants and vegetation again, and the rivers to reclaim a grip on their banks. As a result, erosion was curtailed and the waterways meandered less—all because of an animal that was hunted as a rule by the government and absent from Yellowstone for some seventy years. In some states since, wolf hunting among viable populations has become part of the ruling order for guides and hunters alike; in places like Alaska or Canada, wolves have never been governmentally protected from being hunted.

Some scientists dispute this trophic cascade, arguing that it ignores the fact that while wolves have killed and eaten the elk, the burgeoning bison population is doing the same damage said to have been stopped by the wolves' predation. But the fact remains that this famous park has changed, and in many ways for the better.

It's innate for us to chase that which we love, for love activates our sense of adventure. We can both fear and love animals, but, ultimately, we must be aware of our place within their larger ecosystem. Perhaps our biggest fear is imagining the future, predicting that these creatures will disappear from the landscape—or, a scarier thought, that they won't: that they will still inhabit the earth long after we've gone.

15

THE HUNTER'S LUCK

If the hunter wears rose-colored glasses through which to see his providence, these same glasses cannot shade him from the glare caused by bad luck. So how does the hunter overcome that which prevents him from having the success he so greatly desires?

It may be as simple, and silly, as the good luck charm or token.

Some, like myself, carry an old shell casing as a reminder of a past glory; others an arrow or an article of clothing that their dear ones once wore. If it's not a physical object, it may be a prehunt ritual. He may inspect all of his gear in the same way every time, looking for something that is amiss—maybe his gloves or hand warmers weren't packed—then he'll inspect it again, feeling that he didn't look at it well enough the first time. I like to put my gun out in the garage the night before a hunt so that it acclimates to the temperature, partly because I use a scope but also for the odd reasoning that I feel like my gun likes it outdoors.

Short of casting spells for hunters, charms have a way of matching each hunter's personality. While many may carry similar tokens, they become individual to each hunter and his personal idealization. Take the case of Patrick Meitin, a widely published writer and veteran bowhunter who has related an experience of inspecting one of his many food plots and discovering what is perhaps the most obvious charm there is: an oversized four-leaf clover. Clover, it turns out, is also among the most common attractors of deer, but to Meitin it is also the sign of good things to come. (Although it may be argued that such a veteran bowhunter doesn't need such help in the first place.) Meitin said that he taped the good luck charm to the riser of his bow, and two days later he arrowed a big bear after seeing nothing the entire spring season that year. "What more scientific proof do you need?" he concluded.

There is nothing really special about keeping a four-leaf clover, but if charms such as this one instill in the hunter a confidence that had been missing or had gone awry—as false as it may be—why not take it as truth? Because, as Meitin said, "all future success depends on it."

There's also Dave Hagengruber, who wears a dime-store Buddha charm around his neck that he calls his "lucky genie." The charm was given to him by his wife back in 1987 for a fishing trip, and Hagengruber credits it for saving his life on a fateful floatplane trip that very year when the small bush-jumper aircraft he was in crashed. He survived the wreck and said afterward, "There is no logical reason why anyone was able to live through that."

No logical reason: These words hover over almost every good luck story related by hunters, as though repeating them merits some "logical explanation." If luck is a meal that comes to the hungry hunter, then all hunters get fed a little from time to time. There is no instance in which the hunter comes to this hard-fought windfall without crediting some form of illogical foresight or imagination of what his future might bring, and it all starts with something close to his heart.

If you want the truth, I've been wearing the same exact pair of black sweatpants over my base-layer, fleece thermal underwear, underneath my camouflage hunting cover, for at least the last twenty-five years of my hunting life; the same goes for my faded, off-color T-shirt with purple cuffs and collar, adorned with a horse and rider, surrounded by the words MYRTLE BEACH POLO CLUB emblazoned across the front in capital letters. The pants are wearing thin and have three vertical slash marks on the right thigh where I would wipe the edge of my concrete-finishing trowel on them at work (the trowel would get nicks on its edge from overuse, and these would easily cut into the fabric).

The clothes were provided by my best friend's father, Doug, who was the athletic director at the local high school for many years. In the early summer after school got out, he'd come to the job site where we were working as masons with bags of clothes left over from that years' students. There is no better clothing for the masonry trade than that which is expendable, and the bounty he shared was a Godsend for me and the rest of his son's crew with whom he shared it.

Reuse and Recycle: That was a core philosophy of not only Doug's clothing drop but of his hunt as well. He was a generous and selfless soul while in the woods, and he evinced a veritable kindness. He never got too high when he dropped a buck, and he never complained if he didn't. He was as good a hunter as I ever met; he was never prone to letting any kind of pressure get to him afield, and he wore this trait in life as well.

In 1999 he died abruptly on a pheasant hunt with his son, departing the world for the greater hunting grounds that awaited him, but not before leaving a lasting effect on me. Every time I put those pants and shirt on, I am reminded of his goodwill and his love of the hunt. And despite how worn they are, I can't go without them. State of mind is a powerful force, and carrying a piece of history—a memento of the past—transports a great deal of weight where our future is concerned.

Native Americans—those proud and spectacular hunting souls—learned by watching and reading how the animals of the wilderness adapt themselves to the ways of their prey. Some Cheyenne believed that if they wore a part of an animal they became one with its spirit and were granted some of the animal's powers: Turkey feathers gave them keen eyesight, and bear claws granted strength. The spiritual value of wearing feathers is great among Native Americans, who use them to honor distinct places or as part of their cherished ceremonies. Eagle feathers, which symbolize strength and honor, are the most prominent; while in some cultures, a white one represents an angel that tells of loved ones in heaven who are safe.

Prayer before the hunt and after the kill was compulsory, and modern-day hunters have found themselves doing the same, regardless of their religiosity. Beyond praying for a safe hunt or simple success, the hunter wants to learn something: Did he see his game due to his great awareness, or because he was just lucky? Or is this just his way of justifying the animal's death and dealing with the grief?

Not all religious rites of hunting are created equal. In his book *On the Hunt: The History of Deer Hunting in Wisconsin*, Robert C. Willging discusses how the Chippewa living around Lake Superior hunted: "When game was scarce and hunting success elusive, Ojibwe medicine men would create potions to attract game." He adds that the Ojibwe would never be so brazen as to sharpen their knives before a hunt, fearing that this overconfidence would doom it. These peoples also held that an owl hooting at any time during a hunt spelled disaster for that hunt and was considered a "bad omen." It's apparent that even the most pragmatic Indian hunters would have had a need for some kind of divine intervention. (On opening day of the New York firearms season in 2016, I encountered a loudly hooting owl on my way into the woods. By first light, however, the crows had long since chased it out, leaving the woods that I was hunting as barren as a desert.) Strangely, other Native American nations saw the presence of an owl as a positive sign of wisdom and agility.

Are some hunters just more fortunate than others? Modern hunting personalities such as Jim Shockey, Michael Waddell, and Tom Miranda, to name a few, are in the eyes of many among the "luckiest" hunters known to the outdoor community, despite their hard work and many years of experience. Though it seems a moot point to look only as far as television to answer that question, University of Hertfordshire psychology professor Richard Wiseman found that lucky people tend to have a significantly higher degree of extroversion. Wiseman's *The Luck Factor* argues that lucky people smile twice as much and engage in greater eye contact. They have a higher sociability, which increases their likelihood of obtaining opportunities because they meet so many people, connect better with strangers, and, most important, maintain these relationships. On the other hand, those who are unluckier tend to have a higher rate of anxiety, and "research has shown that anxiety disrupts people's ability to notice the unexpected," thus perhaps blinding the hunter to other opportunities such as that deer walking quietly through the swamp instead of down the obvious trail.

The "famous" hunters mentioned above are well known in the hunting world through their exploits on television, a medium so obviously propelled by extroverted personalities it may make us think that all who are on it have earned some sort of luck by virtue of being on it in the first place. It surely stands to reason that they are outgoing, personality-driven people who, as Wiseman wrote, "are skilled at creating and noticing chance opportunities, make lucky decisions by listening to their intuition, create self-fulfilling prophesies via positive expectations, and adopt a resilient attitude that transforms bad luck into good."

Perhaps the rest of us should focus less on being extroverted and more on the secrets of our own personal accomplishments. Since the average hunter cannot always travel the world as the pro does, it behooves him to rely even more on his sense of what created his most constant luck: his guile and the lessons that experience teaches him. He has his clover, his arrow, and his treasured piece of clothing, but it's his inner belief—the only source of luck that he truly commands—that spurs the most success.

THE HEART AND SOUL
OF SUCCESS AND FAILURE

The harvest is defined as the hunter's yield from nature, the physical return on his efforts and the procurement of meat from any game animal. The feeling he gets upon knowing he has successfully harvested his game is tantamount to his first kiss: He's explored the possibility in his head for a while but was never sure it would happen. Looking back, he still can't quite believe it.

A harvest is a kiss that never comes easy, but once completed it gives rise to unique tales. Some are humble and others more robust in their exultation, but all are voices in the same joyful choir.

A child's first buck, or the first time he ever doubled on a pair of ducks; the first arrow that swimmingly hits the mark, or the initial glimpse of the lifeless deer that was blood-trailed for a hundred yards. Sometimes fondness comes across in the way in which the hunter freely speaks, without hesitation in his voice. The spotlight of success has chosen to shine on him in that moment of recollection, and he has given in to celebration and joy.

And when the tale is over? The hunter's peers are ready to either congratulate him or scoff with unparalleled enthusiasm. He'll either live in the joyful moment forever or forget that his death by failure ever buried him at all. Either way, it's a lofty perch from which to descend.

When I was a teenager, October meant scanning the skies for waterfowl that were finally coming across Lake Ontario on their annual migration south. Since many of my friends and I had just begun to drive, a lot of our free time was spent wasting gas as we maneuvered around the rural farming areas that were not far away from the lake, or from home for that matter. At some point late one October, one of my more adventurous friends came across a group of mallards that had disappeared deep into the middle of the hardwoods, which appeared to be contrary to any ducks' behavior. It wasn't long after my friends and I followed the puddle ducks into the woods that we found a small mysterious swamp hiding there, maybe since the dawn of time. This was so-called flooded timber, the center of many a waterfowl hunter's dreams, a place brimming with dead trees and duckweed. Typically such areas are visible only from the air by group after group of wary, wily, and pond-hopping mallards, which can as easily tip and fly through the branches as they can swim among the bereft trunks of long departed trees, all the while out of sight of the unsuspecting hunter and his shotgun.

By November, after we had been watching the ducks use this swamp for some time—and by then taken a few—the cold that arrived by night had put a thin layer of ice on the water in some parts of the swamp, which crunched when we tried to walk upon it. On one occasion when walking into this wetland, like a sign of grace, a dozen mallards flew in and landed in the only open water some fifty yards away, but it may as well have been five hundred. To stalk these birds wasn't going to be easy, but we had a plan: Two of us would make the treacherous, noisy walk, and one would stay on the outside in the open to try for an easy passing shot as they flushed. For those of us used to sitting down and making sounds with a duck call, hoping to entice puddle ducks, the time came for us to not have much more to do than walk. Yet the ducks were quiet in a way that suggested they had been hunted in the past and now were jumpy. It was a nerve-inducing situation to begin with, but knowing that these wild and skittish birds could break and jump away to safety at any moment made it even worse.

We split up, two of us slowly creaking through the thin ice, pushing it with our knees at first, then our thighs, while our other friend disappeared around the corner to try and head them off.

I had harvested ducks before, but not often in those early days, and the possibility of doing so now seemed paramount. For a young hunter with a wish to stroke his own self-esteem and mark a place in his hunting world as an individual of great import, accomplishment is always met with the weight of consequence: He either watches his fowl drop before the might of his shooting prowess, or he is consumed by the ignominy and shame of the miss. It is wholly lost on the youthful hunter that the best teacher is experience. He is obsessed and never quite seems to see what is necessary before the shot, only that the shot needs to be taken at all costs.

To have lost these ducks that had seemingly come easy would've been inexcusable—nay, *irresponsible*. It would've confirmed my inexperience, my lack of patience and attention to detail. And worst of all, I would have failed in front of my audience of friends.

Now and again the culmination of all the hunter's fears appears before him. This time came in the form of empty water, empty trees, and a lack of sound. I immediately forgot that cunning and silent way to quietly fool my quarry, and I stood up straight and began thrashing through the water, certain that there was nothing there. The dozen or so wild, migrating puddle ducks had covered their tracks by swimming out of the open pool and into the cover of the flooded trees far off to the left, where they decisively flushed the opposite way, out of our reach and never to be seen again. Ignominy my dear, dear friend had come to stay.

For those of us who've struggled to gain this success, and for those who have had only fleeting success, the story is the same: We have gotten to the point of almost giving up before seeing it all change for the better. One of the greatest teachers of success is, of course, failure. If the definition of insanity is doing the same thing over and over and hoping for a different result, then hunters are among the craziest hobbyists in the world.

Hunters rate success in different ways. For some, the amount of time spent licking their hunting wounds, or thinking about what went wrong, is in direct proportion to what the experience taught. The hunter who is the most successful will, without a doubt, spend more time trying to see the positive within the negative, like sifting through sands of time in search of gold, one negative experience collapsing into a million larger ones. Sometimes there's little or no glory in this act.

Back in the early part of the 1980s, I was working on a three-man deer drive with two close friends of mine. The landowner whose property we hunted had told us about the nice buck he had seen cross the road in front of him while he was out for a walk, and how it had disappeared into a thick hummock of trees not all that far from the side of the road. Twenty-four hours later, we set out to see if indeed that buck was hunkered down and waiting out the pressure in this place, where very few people could get to, even during the open deer season. My friend Kevin and I walked around the area, to the west of the hummock, through an old apple orchard that was overgrown by surrounding indigenous weeds and grasses, making a perfect loafing area for deer. I took a stand in the crotch of an old apple tree on one row while Kevin set up just on the high side of the thick little island of trees. A third fellow, John (the same John who had taken me to the North Country beaver swamp), walked in silently from the road. Within five minutes the shooting began. From where I sat I had a great look at Kevin some fifty yards away as he raised his gun and began to unload it on something that I couldn't yet see. It was barely seconds later when I realized I had a front-row seat to a brutish eight-pointer trucking up the row in which I was sitting. Two things rang true for me in that moment: I had accidentally chosen the exact perfect spot in which to sit—and I had made an irresponsible decision that I regret to this very day: I started shooting too. Not that shooting at a big buck during the legal season was regretful, but this deer was fleeing as fast as it could, and I had neither the experience nor competency to ever pull off that shot.

One or both of us hit it, though we'll never know whom. We blood-trailed that deer for hours and found one spot where it appeared to have laid down and bled. But it wasn't there. The trail went cold and we never saw it again.

The positive hunter sees only the next possibility—the shot hitting its mark, the deer that won't escape—while the negative hunter sees only the bloodstain on the ground and all the distance before the next season. So what, then, makes one hunter more successful than another? The hunter who has put in his time has no doubt seen enough unique hunting situations to know that practice and experience is not the only test. Take, for instance, those veteran hunters whose experience into the further reaches of the season will tell you that the deer drive is one of the most important tools for the successful harvest once the pressure of the open season is in full earnest. My friends and I who have done this in areas with a reasonable possibility of success and over many seasons have discovered that the mystery of what the deer will do in certain situations can never be solved. In some instances, they'll comply by running trails, but more often they are more than difficult to predict and will "squirt" out the sides at right angles. Years of exasperating experience have taught us that if we walked more slowly and deliberately, making as little noise as possible, the deer wouldn't so much flee as simply try to avoid us. As a result, we began to find more deer and also predict what might happen. It became apparent by using this slowed-down method that we now had deer that would start off running but would slow to a walk before they got to the hunters on stands waiting for them. We learned through trial and error that animals need to project danger ahead of them, and so by giving them only enough impetus to get moving but not flee into the next county, we would have a realistic chance to see them when the moment of truth arrives.

Some situations proved disappointing but led to satisfying conclusions. One day I moved eighty yards away from the trail that the deer were consistently using and set up on the ground behind a large row of pine trees to ambush the buck that we had been seeing, but only from a distance. As the does scrambled along the trail in the distance—in which I imagined my unused tag going to waste—the chance paid off when an eight-point buck tried to sneak by me. He stopped between myself and the far-off trail, sticking only his head out of the pine row. In the scant seconds that I needed to get my scope with its ready crosshairs on him, he jumped across the limited path and disappeared—a buck not taken, but one that had now shown some of its cards. It's a situation that many experienced hunters foresee and take advantage of, but only by losing out many times first. But not taking the chance is to accept failure without first trying. The success in this situation was not about my slug hitting the mark but about the correct choice made that simply gave my slug the opportunity to hit its mark, *even though the shot was never fired.*

I offer my experiences so that those exposed to similar events will see in hunting a common link. We tell each other these similar stories—lucky ones even—to remind ourselves we're not the only hapless ones out there. It only takes one time to fail, but it takes one hundred to forget the ill-fated moments that live in infamy.

The hunter dares not become complacent lest he revert to his days as a youth, when he felt everything was a given. In the annals of the world of hunting, it shouldn't come as a surprise that up-and-comers expect results, and they expect them now. In many states, there are early youth seasons that give young hunters the first crack at game species that veteran hunters wait all year to chase. Between well-intentioned elders who grant these ambitious youngsters a place at the table—and thus immediate, positive reinforcement—and beginner's luck, it's entirely possible for a young person to have so much early accomplishment that he feels it should always be that way. Without a doubt, if the biggest issue that a youthful hunter has is that he feels somehow entitled to success, then youth hunting seasons are not only a success but necessary. In time will come the inevitable reality that their success is not a given.

In today's world of online sources that supply immediate satisfaction as part of the hunting experience, too many times the young hunter sees the success of others and becomes jaded by it. In the echo chamber of the virtual world, it seems that every hunter has been gifted with perfect luck, and a trophy to coexist alongside it. Elk, turkey, deer, and antelope have now changed their cybernetic first name to YouTube and Facebook.

This is starting to change, though. Many of these online pros are realizing the folly of making it seem like only success is possible and are, instead, starting to share their foibles. They are telling their tales of drudgery and miscalculation that contradict the effort of some in the hunting industry to paint only the rosiest of hunting narratives. This is of great importance to the average hunter. Part of success is the simple feeling that the novice can achieve the same conquest on an equal level as those he looks up to. In my youthful days as a beginner, magazines informed my narrative; hunting shows on television were almost unheard of. The nature photographer was king, and good writing told the rousing story while leaving it to the imagination of the young hunter to pull the trigger in his mind without ever having watched it play out on video.

The problem with today's "entertain me now" world is that it obscures the critical virtues of patience that hunters are desperate to find. Age and time may take their toll on the hunter, but the harvest is the cure. With it he regains spring in his step; the glint in his eye becomes, once more, striking.

———•———

"If the hunter comes back with mushrooms, don't ask him how his hunt was," says a famous Ghanaian proverb. Though I can't recall every single time I came home empty-handed, I can imagine my sallow face and feelings of worthlessness. I can recall lumbering back into my home with the slouch of a child, with a bag containing nothing but void hopes and dreams, with no deer or turkey or pheasant meat to call my own.

If success were an animal it would be a unicorn or an exotic butterfly—a wondrous confluence of space and time, a rarified treat. It would make one yell, "How did I do that?" instead of "Of course I did." Failure is everywhere, like tiny acorns sprouting up through the pine needles. It makes you ask, "Why not?"

Asking questions like this in the first place is part of the hunter's tendency to feel as though he is somehow owed something. In this way, he has already come to the conclusion that his hunting needs have somehow been met and that he doesn't need to put forth the work it takes to be successful.

For others, it's about hitting the wall after careful planning. I can commiserate after considering multiple spring seasons of turkey scouting and seeing the birds in the same place for weeks on end, only to have them completely disappear just a few days before the season opener.

And most discouraging of all? The clean miss: the sound of an arrow skipping off a branch, or the reverberation of a blundered rifle shot that ends in deafening silence. Perhaps it was nerves that caused the misfire: pulling the trigger as opposed to squeezing it, much like letting out the clutch too fast and stalling the car. Misidentifying game can be a mistake of epic proportions, but it's also an inevitability. In the case of waterfowl hunting, it is not always so easy to distinguish drake from hen (in the case of black ducks, it's almost impossible) or one species from another. Ring-necked ducks and bluebills are markedly similar, for instance, and even redheads and canvasbacks can be mistaken for each other in low-light conditions. When in doubt the hunter must be prepared to delay or resist the shot. He is, after all, a creature of habit, but his thought patterns are never quite the same hunt to hunt. He can be both prepared to fire a shot with little or no warning that a bird is coming or on top of him—and resist his normal urge to pull the trigger based on what his eyes relay.

The success of one animal means the failure of another. Any creature that outwits the hunter in any way has won, handing the hunter his subsequent loss. A snow-burrowed grouse might let him walk right by, or it may launch in his face and make him eat snow. Either way, the infrequency of good, solid shooting possibilities at these birds reminds the hunter of how tenuous the chase of any creature is. On the other hand, a mature buck that has survived many hunting seasons *because* of its experience may now, in his older years, let his premier nose get the best of him and walk right in front of you.

Animals aren't so much lucky (like we are) as they are products of their environment. They have adapted to live on what the land has offered them, or they have had to move on to greener pastures. Once these game animals have established themselves in an area, they themselves become the target of other more predatory creatures. Millions of years of evolution have supplied the animal kingdom with a plethora of ways to survive, and it's incumbent upon the hunter to find ways around these natural defense mechanisms. And yet these same animals find many ways around the hunter, who may seem to consider it *unnatural luck*: an animal stopping with most of its body behind a clump of trees; birds flying between brush and branches that seem to have no opening whatever; worst of all, an animal that stops dead at the poorest moment, leaving it hopelessly just out of range. The hunter will be the first to tell you how the wild creatures of the world seem to do everything they expect until the last second. Though he might be able to influence a small portion of the hunt, he is still at the mercy of countless factors out of his control.

The unexpected is as much a part of hunting as it is any part of life. Things that make us fail are the lessons that put us on the path of success, though we don't always understand them as such. Nature is the one constant on which we can rely; and until we realize that failure is a natural part of life, we can only pretend we're successful.

ACKNOWLEDGMENTS

I feel things very intensely at times, and during the writing of this book I felt no differently. All hunters share a passion and drive for the hunt that keeps it inside of our hearts and minds throughout the year. That makes this book for every single one of those who call themselves a hunter.

I first thought about dedicating this book to my son, who had to endure his parents breaking up in 2010 and yet came through with flying colors. His strength at that time was a testament to his fortitude and the type of person that he is deep inside. One of the only ways that I got through it is the fact that we talk almost every day, and in fact, it's the same way that he used to talk to my mother—every single day. Fortunately, he knows what it meant to his grandma to hear his voice on the phone, and especially when he made the effort to visit her. She passed in July 2016. He barely remembers his grandfather, as he passed away in 1997, a man who

ACKNOWLEDGMENTS

loved his grandkids with every inch of his arms and who would have loved the man that he has become. He would have had his grandson out on the boat with a fishing pole as soon as he could handle it, but it was not to be. My parents raised us to love the outdoors and everything about it, so it stands to reason that they weren't the only ones to do so.

All my brother-in-law Steve wanted to do was hunt. Once he and his wife, my sister Connie, took ownership of the sixty acres in Clarkson, New York, he began clearing the property boundaries to make lanes for him and his wife to walk, hopelessly getting lost a few times along the way but enjoying every step. In the chapter "The Heart and Soul of Reflection" it was stated, "There is now community where there was once only undergrowth and resistance, the tracks of new animals that glide by are now customary, not erroneous . . ." This is exactly what happened after their hard work had begun to pay off. As the few years that they had together began to pass here they started to realize just how many animals were using what he so fondly called "the property."

I shot my first wild turkey on the property, and many deer, as did Steve's brother Jeff; Jeff's son Homer (Jeff Jr.); Homer's wife, Heather; Jeff's wife, Barb; Steve's cousin Eddie; and Eddie's son Eddie Jr.; not to mention Jeff's son-in-law Matt. Don't let me forget to mention my nephew John David. It was and is a community of hunters gathered by one man, a group that now hunted with honor thanks to his name and his verve for the hunt.

My dad taught me to fish with a simple bamboo rod when I was so young that I can barely remember it. My earliest recollection was fishing from a rock in Ontario, Canada, at a place called Camp Ge-Kay-Da. Dad said "Pull!" when a fish was biting, and I pulled so hard that the whole mess ended up in the tree behind me, causing some consternation in my father that I'll always remember. My greatest memory of that place revolves around a father-son trip on the boat that only he and I were a part of. Even at that young age I can vividly remember that he was using a yellow rooster tail spinner that had black dots on it. He threw it into some lily pads near the shore, and in a heartbeat, he was hooked up to the biggest walleye that I ever saw.

When we got back to the dock and pulled it out to all the gapes and awes of our family, I'll never forget what he did next—it has stayed with me for my entire life, and I've never told anyone: He told everybody that I caught it! My chest puffed out, my pride swelled to the bursting point, and I never felt as big as I did in that moment. It was the beginning of my love for all things that had to do with the outdoors and all the energy that comes with it.

By the age of ten my mom could easily dispatch and cut up chickens, turkeys, and other small game that her father brought home. I watched her bait her own hook and catch anything that swam, including one damn big smallmouth bass that I still have picture proof of. She was one of the only "girls" I know of that could gut, scale, and cook a pile of fish as fast as you could say it. Both her and her mother could completely debone a northern pike, and as any good fisherman will tell you, that's not easy.

Interestingly enough, neither of my parents ever really hunted. My dad told me stories of his younger days, when he would take his shotgun and walk the nearby fields, and of one man who used to work with him who kept his shotgun in the trunk just in case they saw a pheasant on the ride in. And yet, somehow, it's all I ever remember wanting to do. I read every magazine that I could get my hands on and every book. I watched *The American Sportsman* with Curt Gowdy every week on a TV that you had to actually stand up and walk to in order to change the channel. It was almost exclusively about fishing in those days, with the obligatory quail or pheasant hunt tossed in for good measure. I can recall one week when they were actually going to hunt deer, and I couldn't believe it! Would I truly get to see Curt bag a big whitetail? It turned out that they went on a still hunt: two hunters and a cameraman that kept walking up to the same group, over and over, only to watch the wily deer stay one step ahead of them the entire time. Deer 1, Hunters 0. Even as a little kid I knew that this was just wrong, and there would be nothing for my favorite TV outdoorsman.

I would have to wait many more years before I would get to

see that kind of action on a small screen. Now I can't turn on any of my devices without tripping over it.

You've heard it all before: Hunting is a way of life, it's ingrained in us, it is a part of our history that cannot be denied. That's all well and good and mostly true. The thing is, for me, I can understand that sometimes hunting is the end all reason why we connect to our very nature and can be reenergized by it, but at the same time I realize that it is not always as great as we wish it was. As long as there are poachers and other "takers" who feel the need to put an end to certain animals and call it trophy, thus giving a black eye to the hunt—especially when they post it publicly on social media—then the rest of us will be stuck fighting for our rights against their mockery of the hunt.

When it comes right down to it, I love experiencing the hunt. I never want to look back and say that I didn't give it my all. I can be very vociferous about it or as quiet as snow. I've hooted out loud about it more than once and sat in quiet thought over my kill, both with equal feeling. Without this chance to place my voice next to some of the greats in the hunting community, I would not have had the opportunity to use the storytelling skills that God gave me and that my mother pushed me to use. There are a lot of people to thank, and it starts right here.

Big thanks to my editor, "All Night" Matthew Daddona, who was unafraid to take work home or share the 11:30 p.m. email with me; and to HarperCollins Publishers for sending him to me, possibly by saying, "What about this guy with the shit-eating grin?"

To Mom and Dad, for leaving me four amazing sisters and the best brother ever: Chris, Cindy, Connie, Caren, and Curt (go ahead and laugh now). Forever are they gone but never are they forgotten. To my son, Austin Curtis Raleigh, for the amazing man that he has become, and to his cousins Thomas, Josh, and Claire Alice Raleigh for questioning everything. To Tina, for understanding every single time I disappeared to absorb myself in this project; to Dan and Linda, who gave me their illustrious view of Conley's Lake to work on it. To my "other brother," Kevin Westcott, who taught me so much about the hunt, and his brother "One-Shot" Scott, and especially their dad, Doug, who taught me so much more. To their cousin Big Mike G. for demolishing those adult beverages and for taking his gun for a walk with me, and to Tim and Paul Ainsworth for letting me shoot up their backyard with them. To Tommy and Danny "Three Stitch" Crandall, for being two of the best hunters I ever walked with and for all the severe headlocks that they put me in. To John Farrell and his brother Mike, who opened the door to the North Country beaver swamp, as well as the duck hunting shoals of the mighty St. Lawrence, and invited me to Governor's Island and the enigmatic Zitka for beer and to count shotgun shells. To their parents, Mr.

and Mrs. James (Jim) Farrell, who took to a friendship with my grandparents Tom and Alice Joseph, in a way beyond compare.

And to those grandparents, Thomas and Alice Ellen Swim Joseph, who hunted, fished, and spent their days loving each other while raising eight children, the oldest of which became my mother.

And especially to my Grandpa J., who taught me how to fish, hunt, and swear, all in the same lifetime and all with equal enthusiasm. We would sit in the "little house" together and watch *Gunsmoke*, *Bonanza*, and *Death Valley Days* until our eyes were bleached, all the while intermittently reading *Nebraskaland Magazine* and eating Grandma's lentil bean soup.

And when it was all over, we'd get up, go outside with a flashlight, and catch night crawlers until the sun came up.

These are but a few of the ways that we hunted, and for all of these ways I am grateful.

NOTES AND SOURCES

Chapter Two: OUTDOOR APPRECIATION

27 "the hunting wolf *maheegan* and the bear *makwa*": Barbara Fitzgerald, Pet Helpful, April 21, 2017, https://pethelpful.com/dogs/50-Meaningful-Native-American-Names-for-Male-Dogs.

27 "tendons and parts of the hamstrings": Jacob Broadley, Sciencing, February 9, 2018, https://sciencing.com/cherokee-hunting-traditions-8801.html.

Chapter Three: CONSERVATION

33 "The money taxed from outdoorsmen and women": Rocky Mountain Elk Foundation, January 2013, http://www.rmef.org/Conservation/HuntingIsConservation/25ReasonsWhyHuntingIsConservation.aspx.

34 "Aldo Leopold": Becky Little, National Geographic, July 30, 2015, https://news.nationalgeographic.com/2015/07/150730-cecil-the-lion-hunting-wildlife-conservation-teddy-roosevelt-audubon/.

34 "Theodore Roosevelt": Theodore Roosevelt, *Outdoor Pastimes of the American Hunter* (1905), in *Outdoor Life*, May 28, 2008, https://www.outdoorlife.com/blogs/newshound/2008/05/jrs-random-outdoor-quote.

34 "European eyes looked west to Canada": *Alexander Henry in His 1809 Journal*, in Digital Library, http://digital.library.mcgill.ca/nwc/history/01.htm.

37 "National Wildlife Federation understands": National Wildlife Federation (2018), https://www.nwf.org/sportsmen/about.

39 "bird population in New York": New York Department of Environmental Conservation (2018), http://www.dec.ny.gov/animals/7062.html.

40 "National Wild Turkey Federation": National Wild Turkey Federation (2018), http://www.nwtf.org/about.

Chapter Five: THE HUNTER AS DETECTIVE

58 "numerous Wildlife Management Areas (WMA)": New York Department of Environmental Conservation (2018), http://www.dec.ny.gov/outdoor/7768.html.

59 "High Tor WMA": New York Department of Environmental Conservation (2018), http://www.dec.ny.gov/outdoor/24439.html.

62 "Ornamental and colorful birds": Pheasants Forever (2018), http://www.owendenny-pheasantsforever.org/about.html.

Chapter Six: PRACTICE AS A PURPOSE

78 "legendary Davy Crockett": Aileen Wells Parks, *Davey Crockett: Young Rifleman* (1949), Google Books, 2018, Simon and Schuster, p. 155, https://books.google.com/books?id=eZzPHhR-EI4C&pg=PA155&lpg=PA155&dq=davy+crockett+shooting+contest&source

=bl&ots=rcf2GPGySJ&sig=vyXruVVYSX00wAaj57KonVBE03w
&hl=en&sa=X&ved=0ahUKEwjEvoXjiIjZAhVs_4MKHVdVD7w
Q6AEIUTAK#v=onepage&q=davy%20crockett%20shooting%20
contest&f=false.

Chapter Seven: HOW NATURE HUNTS

81 "tamed Table Rock Lake": Gene Hornbeck, Missouri Department of Conservation, May 2, 2005 (revised Nov. 17, 2010), https://mdc.mo
.gov/conmag/2005/05/table-rock-crawdads.

84 "well known that whitetail bucks": Bob Robb, Grand View Outdoors, September 1, 2014, https://www.grandviewoutdoors.com/big
-game-hunting/why-do-deer-shed-their-antlers/.

Chapter Nine: THE MOST DIFFICULT GAME

100 "Even those two revered figures in American history": Thomas Jefferson Encyclopedia, (no date), https://www.monticello.org/site/house
-and-gardens/elk-antlers.

100 "Of the thirteen different game animals": Lewis and Clark Trail, 2011, http://lewisandclarktrail.com/hunting.htm.

101 "In 2013, it became more than just a legend": John Branch, *New York Times*, February 16, 2017, https://www.nytimes.com/2017/02/16
/sports/bighorn-sheep-hunting.html.

101 "As it is, the bighorn sheep": Utah Division of Wildlife Resources, August 28, 2014, https://wildlife.utah.gov/hunting/biggame/pdf
/2014/14_desert_bighorn.pdf.

102 "If money talks it speaks volumes": John Branch, *New York Times*, February 16, 2017, https://www.nytimes.com/2017/02/16/sports/big
horn-sheep-hunting.html.

102 "Intense trophy hunting for bighorn sheep": Jennifer Pascoe, PHYS.org,

January 22, 2016, https://phys.org/news/2016-01-intense-trophy-artifi
cial-evolution-horn.html.

104 "Take the wild sheep as an example again": John Branch, *New York
Times*, February 16, 2017, https://www.nytimes.com/2017/02/16/sports
/bighorn-sheep-hunting.html.

Chapter Ten: OUR BODIES AS HUNTERS

108 "In 1924, the 2.8-million-year-old skull of a young child, dubbed
the Taung Child": Smithsonian Museum of Natural History, Human
Origins, Revised March 30, 2016, http://humanorigins.si.edu/evi
dence/human-fossils/fossils/taung-child.

108 "Stanford University historian Adrienne Mayor": Paul A. Trout,
Deadly Powers: Animal Powers and the Mythic Imagination, Salon,
December 3, 2011, Prometheus Books, 2011, https://www.salon
.com/2011/12/03/the_evolution_of_monsters/.

Chapter Eleven: ARROGANCE OF THE POACHER

119 "In the forests of Wisconsin": Meg Jones, *Milwaukee Journal Sen-
tinel*, April 6, 2017, https://www.jsonline.com/story/news/2017/04/06
/thousands-birch-trees-have-been-poached-northwoods/100034902/.

119 "In California": Anna Vallery, One Green Planet, February 18, 2015,
http://www.onegreenplanet.org/environment/plant-poaching/.

120 "The Northern Arapaho tribe in Wyoming": *Chicago Tribune*, May
13, 2016, http://www.chicagotribune.com/news/nationworld/ct-bald
-eagle-killings-indian-tribe-religion-20160513-story.html.

120 "In 2014, four men were charged": Mike Porras, Colorado Parks
& Wildlife, July 12, 2016, http://cpw.state.co.us/aboutus/Pages/News
-Release-Details.aspx?NewsID=5836.

121 "For instance, full-sized robotic deer": David Smith, Wide Open

Spaces, February 23, 2018, http://www.wideopenspaces.com/robotic -deer-bears-elk-even-foxes-help-catch-poachers/.

122 "Six different people were caught in Skagit County, Washington": staff writer, Q13 FOX, http://q13fox.com/2018/01/04/poachers-be ware-robot-deer-are-roaming-our-woods-hunting-for-you/.

122 "In New York, the state Department of Environmental Conservation": Craig Raleigh, Wide Open Spaces, October 31, 2015, http://www .wideopenspaces.com/new-york-state-dec-uses-pheasant-decoy-net-ille gal-hunters-pics/.

123 "In early 2017, ten people were arrested": Travis Smola, Wide Open Spaces, May 3, 2017, http://www.wideopenspaces.com/100-animals-in cluding-bears-deer-elk-thrill-killed-washingtons-worst-poaching-case -ever/.

Chapter Twelve: THE HEART AND SOUL OF REFLECTION

125 "*Ānāpānasati*": Andrew Olendzki, Barre Center for Buddhist Studies, summer 2009, https://www.buddhistinquiry.org/article/mindful ness-of-breathing-anapanasati-sutta-mn-118/.

126 "In the early 1980s": Ephrat Livni, Quartz Media, October 12, 2016, https://qz.com/804022/health-benefits-japanese-forest-bathing/.

127 "Take for instance *phytoncides*": Wikipedia, last revised May 7, 2017, https://en.wikipedia.org/wiki/Phytoncide.

127 "Their effect on the human body": Ephrat Livni, Quartz Media, October 12, 2016, https://qz.com/804022/health-benefits-japanese-forest -bathing/.

Chapter Thirteen: FOR LOVE OF THE GAME HARVEST

138 "In more modern times, the nomadic Beothuk people": Ingeborg Marshall, Heritage Newfoundland and Labrador, revised February,

2012, http://www.heritage.nf.ca/articles/aboriginal/beothuk-hunting
.php.

Chapter Fourteen: LOVING ANIMALS VS. FEARING ANIMALS

144 "wildlife authorities in Alligator Point": Kate Good, One Green Planet, November 9, 2016, http://www.onegreenplanet.org/animals andnature/man-rescues-black-bear/.

145–146 "late October 2017": MTN News, KTVQ, October 31, 2017, http://www.ktvq.com/story/36725947/grizzly-bear-attacks-elk-hunter -guide-in-wyoming.

146 "Montana man had the same": Brett French, Montana Untamed, November 6, 2017, http://montanauntamed.com/hunting/article_35b8a09f -c8da-55c6-82c2-2ce0e581a59a.html.

148 "*trophic cascade*": Wikipedia, last revised February 3, 2018, https:// en.wikipedia.org/wiki/Trophic_cascade.

149 "'how wolves change rivers'": Paul Steyn, National Geographic, February 16, 2014, YouTube, February 13, 2014, https://blog.national geographic.org/2014/02/16/this-will-shatter-your-view-of-apex-preda tors-how-wolves-change-rivers/.

149 "Some scientists dispute this trophic cascade": J.D. King, *The Patriot Post*, July 24, 2015, https://patriotpost.us/commentary/36587-wolves -dont-change-rivers.

Chapter Fifteen: THE HUNTER'S LUCK

152 "Take the case of Patrick Meitin": Patrick Meitin, Realltree, July 27, 2012, https://www.realtree.com/brow-tines-and-backstrap/bowhunt ing-and-lucky-charms.

152 "There is nothing really special": Ibid.

152 "There's also Dave Hagengruber": Dave Hagengruber, *Outdoor Life*, December 2, 2014, https://www.outdoorlife.com/articles/2014/12/lucky
-charms-happy-buddha.

154–155 "Some Cheyenne believed": Patrick Durkin as told by Judy Kovar,*Madison State Journal*,September 12,2014,http://host.madison.com
/sports/recreation/outdoors/patrick-durkin-good-luck-charm-pays-im
mediate-dividends-on-elk/article_2eef97dd-0e3e-5781-be21-f9847d
debb45.html.

155 "In his book *On the Hunt: The History of Deer Hunting in Wisconsin*": Robert C. Willging, *On the Hunt: The History of Deer Hunting in Wisconsin*, December 18, 2008, Google Books, Wisconsin Historical Society Press, p. 22, https://books.google.com/books?id=z23yPUYIkyoC&pg=PA2
2&lpg=PA22&dq=deer+hunting+good+luck+charms&source=bl&o
ts=n-awB9u-#v=onepage&q=deer%20hunting%20good%20luck%20
charms&f=false.

156 "University of Hertfordshire psychology professor Richard Wiseman": Richard Wiseman, *The Luck Factor*, May/June 2003, p. 3, http://www
.richardwiseman.com/resources/The_Luck_Factor.pdf.

156 "It surely stands to reason": Ibid.

ABOUT THE AUTHOR

Craig Raleigh grew up hunting and fishing in New York State and Ontario, Canada. A conservationist at heart, he lives for the chance to get outside and discover possibilities, and his lifelong interest in everything outdoors garnered in him a deep respect and love for all living things. He can sit in a tree from dawn to dusk, walk upstream for big Steelhead, hike the Niagara Gorge, or bike the St. Lawrence Seaway Trail and describe to you every detail. He is a senior writer at Wide Open Spaces, one of the Internet's most popular outdoors and hunting websites.